Bought
at Siregh
after weekend in
Wasdale June 2022

THE NATURE LOVER'S BUCKET LIST

RICHARD MADDEN

THE NATURE LOVER'S BUCKET LIST

Britain's Unmissable Wildlife

National Trust

First published in the United Kingdom in 2022 by
National Trust Books
43 Great Ormond Street
London
WC1N 3HZ

An imprint of Pavilion Books Group Ltd

Volume © National Trust Books, 2022
Text © Richard Madden, 2022
Illustrations by Sara Mulvanny/agencyrush.com 2022

ISBN: 9781911657392

A CIP catalogue record for this book is available from the British Library.

10 9 8 7 6 5 4 3 2 1

Reproduction by Rival Colour Ltd, UK
Printed and bound by Toppan Leefung Ltd, China

This book can be ordered direct from the publisher at the website:
www.pavilionbooks.com, or try your local bookshop. Also available at
National Trust shops or www.nationaltrustbooks.co.uk

MIX
Paper from
responsible sources
FSC® C104723

Contents

Introduction

From Madagascar to the Galapagos, islands have long been a source of fascination for naturalists. In each case their physical isolation, coupled with a particular combination of landscape and climate conditions, has resulted in the development of a unique and complex ecosystem. Britain is no exception. Relative to their size, Britain's islands are among the most geologically varied in the world. The sheer diversity of different landforms, from mountains to marshes, gives rise to remarkable biodiversity. After all, where else can you see – theoretically at least! – a golden eagle, a natterjack toad, a basking shark and a hedgehog all on the same day?

Island wildlife has been vulnerable to human influence, too, seeing the arrival of different species and diseases over the centuries, along with the ever-ruthless advance of deforestation, development and climate change. Despite the encroachments of modern times, however, there are still numerous nature reserves and areas of wilderness scattered around Britain's islands. Many are under the protection of conservation charities such as the National Trust. Some are pursuing rewilding projects that have already achieved stunning success: the reintroduction of 'keystone' species such as the beavers at Holnicote Estate in Somerset, for instance, and the breeding programme for Scottish wild cats at the Alladale Estate in the Highlands.

This book celebrates Britain's most charismatic flora and fauna, as well as its most biodiverse nature reserves and wild spaces. Many of the species are relatively easy to see when armed with the right knowledge; others, which a few decades ago were commonplace in our countryside, are now much more elusive and need to be sought out. Among these are many of the 59 species of butterfly that can be seen on our shores, and the glow worms which once so plentifully illuminated our rural hedgerows in high summer. Some of the species are genuinely rare, or confined to certain areas of the country.

While many of us will have experienced the hairs-on-the-back-of-the-neck thrill of seeing a murmuration of starlings forming molten shapes of abstract art against a blood-red winter sunset, few will have been lucky enough to see the dark flash of an otter as it slides, gracefully, into a river, or the endearing face of a pine marten peering out shyly from a hole in a tree. There is something hugely special about witnessing these creatures in their natural habitat.

This book is not only a guide to the species that can still be seen on our islands, but also an invitation to appreciate afresh the experiences and sights that we too often overlook in our quest for the new and exotic. Listening to the dawn chorus in a bluebell wood on a sunny spring morning may not seem extraordinary, but only because an estimated 50 per cent of the world's bluebells are to be found on our islands. Bucket lists are about seeking out new experiences, but this one aims to show you that, for some of the most breathtaking ones, you needn't look very far at all.

I hope that this book will inspire you to rediscover a sense of wonder at the natural history of the British Isles. Our relationship with nature, in all its infinitely varied forms, was at the philosophical heart of the Romantic movement in the early years of the 19th century – an antidote to the new technologies of the Industrial Revolution as they wrought havoc on the natural landscape. As Lord Byron wrote in *Childe Harold's Pilgrimage* (1812):

> *There is a pleasure in the pathless woods,*
> *There is a rapture on the lonely shore...*
> *I love not Man the less, but Nature more.*

Could it be that we are in the middle of such a transformation in awareness, at this present historical moment? Genuine appreciation of the natural treasures that are still ours to enjoy can only fuel our collective determination to halt the decline in populations of our native species. This book, in its own small way, is an attempt to do exactly that.

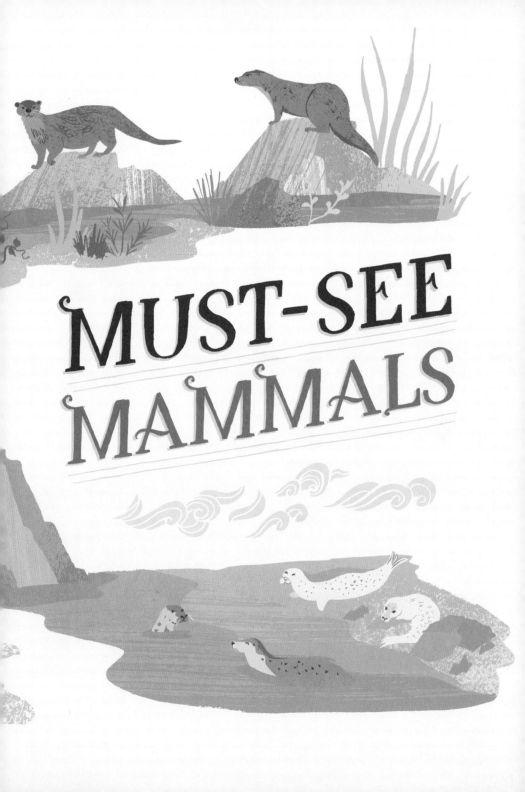

MUST-SEE
MAMMALS

Grey Seal Pups

Beauty and the Beast

As altercations between neighbours go, this one is obviously quite serious. Even at a distance there is an audible succession of angry moans and bellows, and my binoculars reveal a bright red scarf of blood smeared around the neck of one of the participants. Then, as I scan the scene of the aggressors and their watching families, my eyes are drawn to a pair of the most beguiling, mournful and vulnerable eyes I have ever seen.

During the first three weeks of their lives, grey seal pups are utterly defenceless. Unable to swim and protected from the elements only by their fluffy white coats, they are completely dependent on their mothers. One of the many hazards that will assail them during their first year, when only

50 per cent will survive, is being crushed to death by fighting adults, namely a confrontation between two testosterone-fuelled bulls.

Happily, this was not the case on this occasion, and the storm subsided as quickly as it blew up. Breathing a sigh of relief, my fellow seal watchers and I returned to enjoying the uplifting sight of around 10,000 grey seals spread out as far as the eye can see around the shingle spit at Blakeney Point in Norfolk, Britain's largest seal colony. Blakeney is famous for its mixed colony of harbour (common) and grey seals, the former giving birth in June and July, while the greys come ashore between late October and mid-January.

It's a chilly day in early November and I have joined a red-cheeked group of excited wildlife watchers on board one of the small boats that run from nearby Morston Quay to see this annual spectacle. It is one of Britain's greatest wildlife success stories of recent years, with the number of seal pups born each year at Blakeney growing from just 25 in 2001 to over 3,000 today according to the National Trust, which cares for the site.

For seals, giving birth is fraught with hazards, as they are so vulnerable on land. They compensate for this by finding safety in numbers and packing all

their breeding activity into their short sojourn on the coast. The pups are born within days of coming ashore, their mothers having been pregnant for just over 11 months. The birth of the first pup signals to the males it's time to 'haul up'. The weaning process takes three weeks, with the pups feeding on their mothers' rich milk as they triple in size and gradually shed their white fur. Before heading out to sea once more, the females mate with the males and do not return to land for another year.

All this comes at a cost. During their time ashore, neither the male nor female adults are able to feed and can lose up to 40 per cent of the blubber that both sustains them and provides protection from the elements. After they have been weaned, the pups too live off their blubber, until hunger drives them into the sea in search of a meal.

In England, large numbers of grey seal pups can also be seen at Donna Nook Nature Reserve on the coast of Lincolnshire, and on the Isles of Scilly in Cornwall and the Farne Islands in Northumberland. In Wales, the islands of Skomer and Ramsey off the Pembrokeshire coast are important sites, while in Scotland, the Orkneys and the Outer Hebrides attract large numbers.

Hedgehogs

A Prickly Character

If you were to read a description of a hedgehog without actually seeing one, you may not be inclined to regard it with much affection. Its trademark overcoat is made up of over 5,000 spines that are as sharp as needles. When it senses danger, it makes no attempt to escape, but rolls up into a ball – this is not one of nature's more cuddly creations. It also has a penchant for eating slugs, snails, beetles and millipedes (not everyone's idea of a tasty snack) and its black, sausage-shaped droppings often retain the undigested body parts of insects.

Hedgehogs are not very sociable, hiss if they are annoyed and often make strange grunting and snuffling sounds, rather like a pig. They are solitary, and only usually meet up with other members of their species during the mating season between May and September, an activity that is accompanied by a noise reminiscent of the chuffing of a steam train. Females are left to bring up baby hedgehogs – known as hoglets – on their own. Hedgehogs spend a lot of time sleeping, hibernating between November and early April, depending on the temperature. When they do finally venture out of their nest when the weather warms up, it's almost always after dark.

Everyone knows a few humans who fit this description rather well: prickly characters with rather unsavoury habits. But to watch a hedgehog, with its long, pointed nose, round ears and short legs, scuttling across your lawn and into a hedgerow, before emerging clutching grasses and twigs for its nest, is to fall in love with this harmless, charismatic creature.

Despite the fact that hedgehogs are regularly voted Britain's favourite mammal, human activity has had a terrible impact on our prickly friends over the last few decades. At least one-third of their population has been lost in the last 20 years, much of this due to the destruction of their natural habitat.

Hedgehogs, as their name suggests, love hedges, which provide protection, food and corridors for moving around. They are often found in fields and woodlands, but they also love gardens. However, traffic, pesticides, netting, open drains, hedge and grass strimmers, hedge removal and bonfires – among other factors – have all contributed to falling numbers. The habit of dividing urban environments into smaller and smaller areas has also made it increasingly difficult for our spiky friends to roam the distances they need – more than 1 mile (1.6km) every night – to find food, a mate and to survive.

The good news is that organisations such as the British Hedgehog Preservation Society and the People's Trust for Endangered Species have mounted highly successful campaigns to raise awareness of the hedgehog's plight. New housing developments often include hedgehog-sized holes in garden fences to create 'hedgehog highways' through neighbourhoods. Many households now build hedgehog houses in their gardens or create log piles where they can nest, while leaving out food (wet cat or dog food will do) and water at night. Though remember to never give them milk, as hedgehogs are unable to digest lactose. Developing a network of hedgehog-friendly gardens will play a significant role in helping to reverse the decline of this delightful animal.

Red Squirrels

A Magical Tail

We are all familiar with the daring aerial antics and high-energy activity of both red and grey squirrels. But it is the red squirrel, with the burnished radiance of its russet-coloured fur, its tufted ears and the luxurious extravagance of its tail that tugs at the heart strings. Red squirrels (*Sciurus vulgaris*) have lived in the UK for around 10,000 years.

Grey squirrels (*Sciurus carolinensis*) were introduced from North America to about 30 sites in the UK between 1876 and 1929. The greys brought with them a virus called squirrel pox, which they carry with no harmful effects but can pass on to the reds, who have no natural resistance to this fatal disease. Greys are also prolific breeders, often producing two litters every year. The combined

effect of these factors has been the near eradication of red squirrels from the south of Britain.

One of the most beloved physical characteristics of a squirrel is its tail, particularly the red's long, bushy version. As well as the visual appeal of its curling, bouncing exuberance, a squirrel's tail is vital to its survival and used for multiple purposes, including balance, temperature control, communication and protection from both predators and the elements. Vigorous tail-flicking is observed in many social interactions, while males also use them to attract a mate.

Squirrels seem to appreciate the idea of keeping something for a rainy day – or in their case, a winter's day. Their broad-based diet includes berries, nuts, fungi, pine seeds and pine cones. The greys are also able to eat acorns, though the reds are unable to digest them due to their high tannin content. The nuts they bury on the forest floor (known as caching) are located by smell, but they are just as likely to find a store hidden by one of their neighbours.

Red squirrels favour coniferous and broadleaved woodland. They spend most of their time up in the canopy; as they scurry through the treetops, a fleeting glimpse of their exhilarating high-wire antics is a rare treat of acrobatic skill. Reds are equally at home – and often easier to see – scampering along the forest floor in September and October when they are collecting food to sustain them during the winter.

Around 75 per cent of the UK population is to be found in Scotland, with other strongholds in the Lake District (Borrowdale, Aira Force, Allan Bank) and Northumberland (Wallington Estate). Smaller groups in England and Wales can be found on the Isle of Anglesey (Wales), Brownsea Island (Dorset) and the Isle of Wight. There is also a red squirrel walk in the coastal pinewoods on the Sefton Coast at Formby, near Liverpool. Populations can also be found in Northern Ireland on the north-east coast of Antrim, the Fermanagh Lakelands of Crom, the Mourne Mountains and Mount Stewart on the Ards Peninsula, County Down.

Beavers

Nature's Eco-engineers

Beavers are one of the UK's most charismatic creatures. Their pointed, inquisitive faces, outsized noses, buck teeth, twitching whiskers and energetic temperament rank them high on the list of the nation's favourite animals. When the first beaver in 400 years was born at the National Trust's Holnicote Estate on Exmoor in 2021, it made front-page news.

During medieval times, beavers were widespread in our rivers and waterways, but by the 16th century had been hunted to near extinction. Their thick pelt with its red-brown outer layer over an inner layer of dense, soft finer hairs was highly prized as a material for making hats and coats. The oil (castoreum) they secrete as a territorial marker and whose waterproof qualities help keep them dry, was also used in a number of medical treatments.

The reintroduction of beavers to Scotland in 2009 after an absence of several centuries was supported by a number of environmental organisations. Beavers are now defined as a 'keystone' species, in that their presence has a major effect on the surrounding ecosystem and stimulates biodiversity.

Beavers are renowned for their impressive engineering skills, most notably for building dams, connecting canals and creating the 'lodges' where they live and breed. Dams are built to ensure that the entrances to their lodges further upstream remain under water. This protects them from land-based predators, although nowadays, the bears, wolves and lynx that once hunted them are themselves gone from Britain.

The beavers' building work has the effect of regenerating the surrounding ecosystem and creating a mosaic of wetland habitats that attract a wide variety of other species. Sometimes these include endangered animals such as otters and water voles, and large numbers of invertebrates, birds, plants, fungi, frogs, toads and fish, some of which are also threatened. The materials used include everything from tree branches to rocks, mud, grass and plants.

Their dams help clean rivers of pollutants, including pesticides, as well as reducing the water flow after heavy rain and thereby lowering the chance of flash-flooding further downstream. Conversely, beaver activity can also impact land drainage by raising water levels, which can potentially bring their presence into conflict with some land management practices. This is one reason why beavers can only be legally reintroduced under licence. However, as well as small Scottish licensed populations in the Knapdale Forest in Argyll, there are also unlicensed populations in the Tay and Forth catchments.

When beavers of unknown origin started breeding in the River Otter in Devon, a five-year study was undertaken to monitor their effects on the landscape, and in 2020 the decision was made that the beavers could stay. The best place to see them is from footpaths that run close to a river bank. As beavers are primarily nocturnal animals, they are most easily spotted on long summer evenings between May and September, with the village of Otterton in East Devon being a particular hotspot.

Beavers have also been reintroduced to the Knepp Estate in West Sussex. Environmental groups, such as Citizen Zoo, also have plans to release beavers in select parts of London.

Otters

Life on the Edge

Some of our fellow creatures have the power to hypnotise. The otter is one of them. When caught in the fleeting moment of a photograph, otters have a lithe and graceful beauty, but it is their movements that cast the spell. Living in a liminal world between land and water, their staccato twists and turns – whether feeding, swimming, hunting for fish and crabs or making a nest – make them one of the most purposeful creatures you will ever encounter.

In the water, otters like to keep a low profile, swimming with their heads just above the surface, unlike seals, which will often bob around with their heads fully exposed. Seen on land, it is the otters' pointed snouts with their grandfatherly faces, graced by long drooping whiskers and snub noses shaped like arrowheads, that entrance us.

The otter's sleek body is covered in two layers of fur. This dense covering – around half a million hairs per square inch – keeps them warm, aids buoyancy and is also perfectly adapted to navigating the treacherous mix of rock, seaweed and surging tides that makes the margin between sea and land so hazardous to other creatures. Their transit between the two, using their webbed feet and a powerful swish of that muscular tail, is as smooth as moving from one room to the next.

The time otters truly wave the magic wand is when playing with and grooming their children and siblings. This cat-like behaviour involves sudden explosions of topsy-turvy madness and play-fighting. Their North Pacific relative, the sea otter, even holds hands with its babies at night to keep them from drifting away while they sleep. They have even been observed wrapping each other in kelp and plants, literally tying themselves together.

In the UK, the revival of the Eurasian otter has been highly successful over recent years. From an all-time low in the 1950s (when the otter disappeared from central and southern England), through a hunting ban in the 1970s and

the improving water quality of our rivers, the otter's range has expanded from its strongholds in the north; it can now be found in every county of Britain, living both on the coast and along inland waterways.

Otters are notoriously difficult to observe in the wild. While tracking them is relatively easy, through their spraint (droppings) and rosette-shaped toe prints, they will disappear in an instant if they smell or hear humans approaching.

Locations with healthy populations in England and Wales include the Somerset Levels (Avalon Marshes); Hampshire (the Itchen and Test Rivers and Winnall Moors, Winchester); East Anglia (RSPB Minsmere); Lancashire (RSPB Leighton Moss); Cumbria (Ennerdale); and Pembrokeshire (Bosherton Lakes and Stackpole Court). Increasingly, sightings are also being reported in our towns and cities.

In Scotland, otters live around many lochs, but the largest populations are located along the west coast (Ardnamurchan Peninsula) and its outlying islands (the Shetlands and Hebrides).

Boxing Hares

March Madness

It is one of the best-loved rites of spring. Standing upright, chest-to-chest on those powerful back legs, whiskers twitching, ears erect, paws scrabbling at breakneck speed. As boxing matches go, hares are in a league of their own.

Immortalised by Lewis Carroll in the tea party scene from *Alice's Adventures in Wonderland* (1865), a crown of broken corn woven comically around his long ears, the Mad March Hare has become a symbol of over-excited and irrational behaviour brought on by an excess of spring fever. Not for nothing are the drunken revellers in the 15th-century poem *Colyn Blowbols Testament* described 'as braynles as a Marshe hare'.

It is a common assumption that the participants in this annual ritual are both males competing for breeding rights. In fact, one – often the larger of the two – will be a female (doe) fighting off a male (buck), either because she is not yet ready to mate, or because she is assessing his suitability as a gene donor for her future offspring. In this instance, she is the one in charge. Each bout can last for two minutes or more, but there is none of the potentially deadly intent of the autumn deer rut. Often the only evidence of the encounter will be small tufts of white fur dislodged from their underbellies floating harmlessly away on the breeze.

Two species of hare live in the British Isles. The brown hare (*Lepus europaeus*) has long, powerful back legs, golden-brown fur, comically elongated, black-tipped ears, white underbelly and a black-topped tail. The pale grey mountain hare (*L. timidus*), whose fur turns white in winter as camouflage against the snow, is smaller; while the Irish hare (*L. timidus hibernicus*) – a subspecies of the mountain hare – has light brown fur, shorter ears and an all-white tail. Brown hares are Britain's fastest land mammal, with a top speed of up to 45mph (72km/h). They live primarily in the lowland arable fields, grasslands and woodlands of East Anglia and the South of England, particularly Wiltshire and Hampshire.

Hares box for much of the year, but being mostly nocturnal, it is much easier to see them in the early morning or evening in March or April. During these early spring months the days are getting longer, and the undergrowth in the fields and woodlands is shorter, making them easier to spot.

The sweeping moorlands of the National Trust's Lyme estate in Cheshire – Mr Darcy's Pemberley residence in the BBC production of *Pride and Prejudice* (1995) – has a thriving population of brown hares, as does the Wimpole Estate in Cambridgeshire, Uwchmynydd on the rugged Llŷn Peninsula in the far west of Wales, and Dunwich Heath in Suffolk.

Other excellent locations for a ringside seat are the RSPB Minsmere Nature Reserve, also in Suffolk, as well as the Peak District – the only location in England with a population of mountain hares, most of which are to be found in the Highlands of Scotland. The rare Irish hare is best seen on Rathlin Island off the coast of County Antrim in Northern Ireland.

Mountain and Moorland Ponies

Wild at Heart

Exmoor, Dartmoor, the New Forest, the Welsh mountains, the Shetlands: each of these famously beautiful parts of the country have given their name to one of the 16 native pony breeds we call 'wild'. While they are all descended from breeds that have been domesticated to some degree or another, and are still managed by humans today, the vast majority of their lives are very wild indeed.

One of the hardiest breeds of all lives in the Carneddau mountains of north-west Wales and is thought to date back to the Bronze Age, around 3,500 years ago. This starkly beautiful wilderness is surrounded by the steep, rocky valleys and 3,000ft (900m) peaks of the Snowdonia National Park. In the summer, the hills are a magnet for walkers and wildlife lovers, but in mid-winter they can be wet, dark and forbidding, with freezing temperatures and high winds.

The rugged lives of the Carneddau ponies are interrupted only once a year in late autumn, when the herd of around 300 are rounded up for health checks, and some of the younger animals are sold off to avoid overgrazing. The ponies that remain are vital to the maintenance of the mountain landscape, keeping bracken and gorse under control through grazing and trampling, while those that are sold often go on to help conserve the health of the ecosystems of their new homes, which include fens, dunes, heathlands and grasslands.

Small numbers of a semi-feral breed from Poland have been introduced to help manage some of the UK's most important wildlife sites. Konik ponies are the closest living breed to the tarpan, an extinct European wild horse depicted in Neolithic cave paintings with the same dun colouring, upright mane and dorsal strip down the middle of its back. In wetland wildlife havens such as Wicken Fen in Cambridgeshire, Konik ponies help keep the landscape biodiverse by grazing on reeds, improving conditions for nesting birds and helping to attract new species of plants and insects.

Another good proxy for extinct wild breeds is the Exmoor pony. Its compact, dark brown silhouette with its shaggy mane blowing in the breeze viewed against a summer sunset on Dunkery Beacon, Exmoor's highest point, is a

memorable sight. Exmoor ponies can also be seen at the Knepp Estate in West Sussex, where their trampling, grazing and defecating is helping the Knepp rewilding project.

In West Cornwall, the National Trust is using Shetland ponies to manage coastal heathland at Rinsey. Britain's smallest horse breed helps prevent the clifftops above this beautiful cove from becoming overrun with bracken and gorse. When the ponies are moved in the spring after a winter of grazing, these tough, sprawling plants no longer dominate the landscape, opening up areas for wild flowers to thrive.

Another project at Cissbury Ring, within the South Downs National Park in West Sussex, has brought in New Forest ponies to keep the thickets of bushes and trees from encroaching on the chalk grasslands. While their natural behaviour can undoubtedly help keep our wildest habitats healthy, wild ponies are also a much-loved sight and a stirring symbol of our British wildernesses.

Autumn Deer Rut

To the Victor, the Spoils

Throughout history, we humans have always played much the same game. Whether it be Roman gladiators, jousting medieval knights or modern heavyweight boxers, all are the theatrical embodiment of the 'survival of the fittest'. But in the case of the annual deer rut, that titanic struggle between the alpha males of the deer species, the reward for the victor is truly Darwinian: the right to pass on their genes to the next generation.

Every autumn, rising to a frenzy in mid-October, horns are locked in forests, moorlands, hillsides and deer parks across Britain, as the males of our three largest deer species (red, fallow and sika), fight it out to decide who will father the next generation. Their weapons are every bit as deadly as our own. The antlers of a red deer male can grow to more than 3ft (almost 1m) in length and weigh more than 3st (19kg), while the fallow deer's broad, palmate antlers resemble the grasping hands of a giant. Both have multiple sharp 'tines' that can rip through flesh with a quick flick of their majestic heads.

Fights most often break out just after dawn and before dusk, frequently making for an atmospheric background to their ferocious duels. It begins with a dominant male, called a stag (reds and sika) or a buck (fallow), rounding up a group of females (does or hinds). This is followed by a series of loud, deep grunts (fallow), bellows (red) or high-pitched whistles (sika), to announce his control of the territory and deter any nearby males daring to challenge his sexual authority.

Meanwhile, testosterone-fuelled pretenders to his throne will be circling around, scraping their antlers against trees, picking up pieces of undergrowth to make them look larger and more threatening. They will also dig holes in the ground, wallow in mud scented with their own urine and make short, darting runs alongside their adversary to test out the opposition.

When the fight begins, heads are lowered as the antagonists charge into battle, their antlers locking together in a violent display of shaking heads, each seeking an angle that will give them a crucial advantage, while at the same time trying to maintain their balance as their foe twists and turns in response. This trial of strength is accompanied by the traditional soundtrack of the deer rut: the frenetic clack-clack-clack of antler on antler.

While fatalities do sometimes occur, the weaker male will usually back down as the victor bellows in triumph and seeks out a responsive female with whom to celebrate. But all this comes at a price. During the rut, the males are rarely able to eat and may lose up to a quarter of their body weight.

Deer parks are the most reliable locations to be sure of witnessing this annual rite, as they are enclosed and often located in historic and inspiring landscapes. These include Lyme in Cheshire, where deer have lived for more than 600 years, Dinefwr in Carmarthenshire and Arlington Court in Devon, all cared for by the National Trust. In London, Richmond Park is home to more than 600 deer (red and fallow), while the Exmoor National Park has 3,000 red deer, including 300 on the Trust's Holnicote Estate in Somerset. In Scotland, the Braes of Glenlivet in the Cairngorms, the Isle of Arran and the Isle of Jura are all excellent options.

Pine Martens

Forest Gymnasts

The agility and charisma of the pine marten are legendary. For anyone who has ever seen one, its twitching, inquisitive snout, prominent round ears and the creamy yellow bib on its throat and chest are instantly recognisable. Its sleek body covered in chestnut-brown fur grows up to around 2ft (0.6m) in length and its tail is long and bushy.

A member of the mustelid family – carnivorous mammals that include the badger and the otter – the pine marten's appearance is more like its smaller relatives, the weasel and the stoat. Their varied diet consists mainly of small mammals, in particular rabbits and squirrels, but they do have a sweet tooth, seeking out seasonal fruits and berries. They also eat birds' eggs, including

those of pheasants, a transgression for which, along with their highly coveted fur, they were almost hunted to extinction.

The pine marten's long, sinuous shape makes it perfectly adapted to the trees in which it spends most of its life. They are extremely effective treetop hunters, twisting like gymnasts in pursuit of squirrels, which are no match for their highly-tuned athleticism. Pine martens are mostly active at night, preferring densely wooded areas with good cover, and are solitary animals with large territories of several square miles.

Recent changes in forest management, particularly in Scotland, have helped the pine marten's resurgence. The reduction of single-species conifer woodland has made forests more diverse, which favours pine martens as they prefer mixed woodlands. Breeding boxes that are resistant to foxes, the pine marten's main predator, have also been left in likely locations for mating.

While pine martens are easiest to spot in the north-west of Scotland and in Northern Ireland, they have recently begun to spread over the border into parts of Northumberland, Cumbria and Yorkshire. They have also been reintroduced into both Mid Wales and the Forest of Dean. This has also benefited red squirrels, which evolved alongside pine martens, and in these areas the greys are in decline as the pine martens bring the population under control.

Because pine martens are nocturnal, they are very difficult to spot in the wild. However, sites where they are most likely to be seen include Glenloy Lodge, north of Fort William in Scotland, where visitors can watch the animals being fed from behind a glass-fronted enclosure; Cwm Rheidol, Ceredigion, in Wales, where the Vincent Wildlife Trust reintroduced the animals in 2014; and the Crom Estate in County Fermanagh in Northern Ireland, where the National Trust are actively encouraging conservation plans to protect the species.

Wild Boar

Friends or Foes?

In 2009, a white boar with fearsome tusks and a mane of bristles running along its back was found in a boggy field in Leicestershire. It soon became apparent that this beast had fought alongside Richard III at the Battle of Bosworth Field in 1485. The white boar was the personal emblem of the king and this silver gilt badge was almost certainly worn by one of his knights. The spot where it had lain for more than 500 years is thought to be where Richard met his end, killed by supporters of Henry Tudor.

At the time of the battle, wild boar were being hunted to extinction in Britain, but its reputation for bravery, strength and ferocity in a tight corner was beyond doubt. Such qualities were widely attributed to Richard himself by both friend and foe.

More than half a millennium later, wild boar are once more roaming free in our woodlands. In the 1980s, boar were farmed for their meat but, using their legendary tenacity, some escaped and established a population of wild animals in southern England. According to the Woodland Trust, around 2,600 of these mighty beasts, the ancestors of our domestic pigs, can be found in mainland Britain. By far the majority of these mammals roam the inner sanctums of the Forest of Dean along the Wales-England border, but there are also groups in Gloucestershire, Wiltshire, Sussex and Dumfries and Galloway.

At more than 3ft (almost 1m) tall and covered in thick, brown-black hair, the wild boar has a huge shaggy head, with small eyes, large ears and blunt snout, which accounts for more than a third of its body length, making its thin legs look relatively insubstantial by comparison. The males are distinctive for the sharp tusks in their upper and lower jaw, which are actually canine teeth. These continue to grow throughout their lives and are sharpened by continual contact with one another as the animal chews and eats.

Despite their fearsome reputation, wild boar are actually very shy and elusive creatures that avoid humans whenever possible. Their reputation for aggression comes as a result of being relentlessly hunted over many centuries. Unless provoked, or their piglets are disturbed, they are extremely unlikely to attack passing walkers and are an impressive sight when seen in their woodland habitat.

Wild boars are omnivores, feeding on everything from acorns, bulbs, berries and nuts, to insects, birds' eggs and small mammals. In extremis, they even hunt calves and lambs. Wild boars are beloved by rewilders as their disturbance of the ground creates new seedbeds which, in turn, stimulates plant biodiversity. Their give-away signatures are the turf scrapes they leave behind in fields, or along the forest floor, which they plough up with their large heads as they forage for food.

When wild boar behaviour causes damage, it understandably leads to conflict with local farmers and landowners. The forests where wild boar have lived for thousands of years are part of our past; let us hope that together we can find a solution so that these animals can remain as part of our future.

Badgers

Heroes or Villains?

Even in children's literature, badgers have been portrayed as both heroes and villains. On one side there is Susan Varley's tender story of a kind old badger that has introduced countless children to the ideas of grief and loss in *Badger's Parting Gifts* (1984). Then there is Bill Badger, comic strip favourite Rupert Bear's optimistic, reliable friend, who is always there for him in times of trouble. On the other is Tommy Brock, Beatrix Potter's curmudgeonly down-and-out who kidnaps Benjamin Bunny's offspring and plans to eat them in *The Tale of Mr. Tod* (1912).

On the face of it, badgers undoubtedly fall into the former group. Widespread throughout Britain, they live in burrows called setts and in extended family groups known as clans. These are typically found on hillsides in woodland surrounded by plenty of undergrowth. Once your eyes are attuned, setts are quite easy to recognise and have often been used for many generations, sometimes over many decades.

The most noticeable feature of a sett is its many entrances, sometimes as many as 40 or 50. These access points tend to be surrounded by large mounds of soil covered with vegetation that has been used as bedding material. Underground will be an impressive network of tunnels connecting the chambers where the badgers live and sleep during the day. Other telltale clues to a badger's presence are their paw prints, usually with four out of their five claws visible at the front. There is frequently a well-worn badger highway winding its way across the woodland floor.

Badgers are famously nocturnal animals, so the best chance of observing them is when they embark on a night's foraging. Early February is a good time for badger watching as the young have just been born and there is usually a lot of scrabbling around with bedding materials in close proximity to the sett. Understandably, most people opt for spring when it's sometimes possible to see the cubs play-fighting and the adults grooming themselves surrounded by a sea of bluebells.

It is the ritual of leaving their underground refuge that is most compelling. They emerge with a twitching, sniffing nose followed by a retreat inside to report back to the rest of the group, who eventually appear with their cubs in tow. The easiest way to connect with these tough, strong-willed, funny animals is to join a Badger Watch group and observe them in comfort from a hide, knowing that you will not be disturbing them.

So how, you may well ask, can a badger be portrayed as a villain? Badgers are known to eat hedgehogs and bird's eggs, although neither are a significant part of their diet. Sadly, there is also the issue of bovine TB and the science behind how this pernicious disease spreads through dairy herds and threatens the livelihoods of farmers. Some blame the badger, while others, including many scientists, believe the disease is primarily spread through cattle-to-cattle transmission. There are signs that the cull, which started in 2013 and has resulted in the deaths of more than 130,000 badgers and cost more than £60 million, may be coming to an end, although as of 2021 this practice continues.

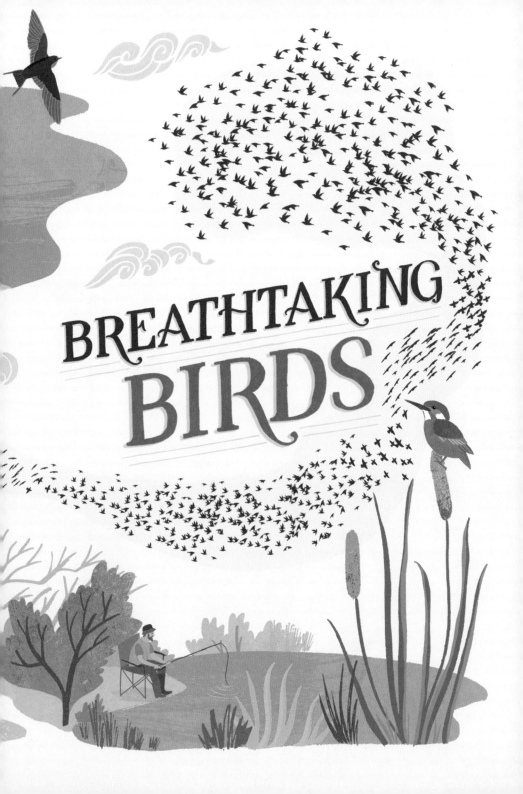

BREATHTAKING
BIRDS

Starling Murmurations

Shape-shifters of the Winter Dusk

It's the sound that is so unnerving. The sudden surge of 50,000 wingbeats, like the muffled drumbeat of an approaching thunder shower, sends my flight or fight response into overdrive. Caught in the downdraught, our small band of wildlife enthusiasts clutch one another with excitement.

This adrenalin rush is soon overtaken by a wave of endorphins, as one of nature's great set pieces unfolds in the sky above. Like abstract art, the shapes defy description. Constantly melting, then thickening, then folding back on themselves, like a dream slipping through the fingers on waking, they dissolve in and out of recognisable shapes so quickly that they are impossible to pin down. But they always remain together: a single organism made up of tens of thousands of birds.

Starling murmurations occur in the UK throughout the winter months, from late October onwards. The birds flock as they come together to roost after a day of foraging in smaller numbers. Murmurations usually peak in January or February, their numbers increased by the many thousands of birds that migrate from continental Europe, in particular Russia, to spend the winter on our shores after the ground becomes too hard for them to forage. Early evening at around 4pm, just as the sun is setting and the starlings are preparing to sleep for the night, usually produces the most electrifying displays.

But why exactly have starlings evolved collectively into such electrifying shape-shifters? Hypnotising humans, it seems, is not the primary purpose; more likely it's to confuse predators such as peregrine falcons, sparrowhawks and buzzards. On clear nights, when the risk of predation is greater, they flock in noticeably larger numbers, as they do during very cold spells when it is thought murmurations help the birds to keep each other warm. But some

starling behaviour is still not fully understood. One example is why, if the birds are trying to avoid predators, they don't roost immediately but instead keep up their displays, even after they have been attacked, sometimes for up to an hour.

Starlings often roost in reedbeds where they are safe from land predators such as foxes, which is why the Avalon Marshes in the Somerset Levels, particularly RSPB Ham Wall, attracts so many murmuration enthusiasts. Other excellent reedbed sites include Wicken Fen in Cambridgeshire, RSPB Leighton Moss in Lancashire and WWT Slimbridge Wetland Centre in Gloucestershire. Piers are also popular with starlings as, like reedbeds, they are located over water and protected from land predators. They also make an excellent backdrop for photographers. The derelict West Pier in Brighton and the Royal Pier, Aberystwyth, are both highly popular murmuration sites.

Atlantic Puffins

Orange-billed Poster Birds

The choice of a puffin on the front cover of a wildlife magazine is one few editors can resist for long. Like the panda, its face seems to have evolved with the specific purpose of melting human hearts. Its technicolour beak looks almost too vivid to be real, while its sleepy-lidded eyes add a final endearing touch to one of nature's most memorable faces.

During summer, these charismatic creatures – members of the auk family (*Fratercula arctica*) – nest on grasslands high above remote sea-cliffs, mainly on Britain's coastal islands. After spending eight months of the year at sea in the harsh conditions of the northern oceans, they return in spring to mate and dig the clifftop burrows where they raise their young.

Largely monogamous, after locating a partner they have not seen for the entire time they have been at sea, puffins greet one another by rubbing their beaks together in a display known as 'billing'. This is another of their characteristics that plucks at the heartstrings and pulls in legions of admirers. They can also reach speeds of 55mph (88.5km/h) in flight and are renowned for their frequent crash landings.

Puffins make their nests in burrows, which they dig out with their feet and beaks, or sometimes inherit from rabbits. Usually around 3ft (0.9m) deep, the burrows are lined with grass and feathers. In late April or early May, the female lays just one egg – a factor that makes their populations vulnerable – which the couple then incubate together for up to 45 days. A rarely heard sound is the call they make in their burrows, like a high-pitched chainsaw.

During the breeding season, the puffins' beaks change from the dull grey of their winter plumage to the bright orange for which they are best known. Their beaks also feature spikes (denticles) along the top of the jaw, which allow them to take more fish while already holding on to a previous catch; puffins can hold around 10 fish in their mouths at any one time.

The puffin is categorised as Vulnerable on the International Union for Conservation of Nature Red List of Threatened Species. Its populations are restricted to a small number of breeding sites and its food supply, which includes sand eels and herring, is susceptible to over-fishing. The best time of year to visit these sites is spring and early summer between March and July. By the end of August, both the newly fledged 'pufflings' and their parents will have departed their nests.

Puffin breeding sites in the UK are mostly offshore; in England and Wales these include the islands of Lundy (North Devon), Skomer (Pembrokeshire) and South Stack (Anglesey), as well as the Farne Islands and Coquet Island off the coast of Northumberland. A notable exception is the precipitous chalk towers of Bempton Cliffs Nature Reserve in Yorkshire, managed by the RSPB and home to one of the UK's most diverse seabird colonies.

In Scotland, the Isle of May in the Outer Firth of Forth, the Orkneys, Shetlands and Hebrides are all excellent puffin-spotting sites; Hermaness Nature Reserve on Shetland is perhaps the jewel in the crown, due to its fabulous cliff views.

The Dawn Chorus

Nature's Signature Tune

If nature did have a signature tune, there could only be one serious contender. With its ever-changing cast and an oratorio rewritten on a daily basis, the dawn chorus is always unique, but also profoundly the same. It is the music of life itself.

Those first chimes of bell-like vibrato, from a soloist perched tiptoe on the top-most rung of the treble clef, are most likely sung by Britain's national bird, the robin. This piercing rendition will be followed in short order by the melodic warble of the blackbird and the polysyllabic twitters and tweets of a long list of celebrity performers including thrushes, skylarks, blackcaps, chiffchaffs, tits, doves and pigeons.

The dawn chorus is one of nature's greatest gifts. The invitation to witness the birth of a new day is open to anyone lucky enough to have access to green space – be it urban park or country woodland – and sufficiently determined to rouse themselves from their slumbers in time to watch the sun rise.

These outdoor promenade concerts are one of the earliest signs that spring has finally arrived. They begin in March and continue until July, with top billing reserved for May and June, when the displays of sound, light and colour are at their most intense. They peak half an hour before dawn and continue until half an hour after the sun has risen – well before the cacophony of daily life has had a chance to intervene.

But is this all just nature's way of shaking us out of our night-time torpor? Not exactly. Evolution, as always, tends to focus on the propagation of life, and the dawn chorus is no exception. Breeding rights, food and territory are the main drivers. The soloists with the loudest songs are sending out a powerful message that they are the strongest and healthiest specimens around, with the best genes to pass on, while also sending a warning to any potential competitors that this territory is already taken. The time of day, when the world

is at its quietest and the air is still, also means that their songs of seduction will carry a great deal further than at midday.

Recent studies by Bernie Krause, the American musician and 'soundscape ecologist', have shown that the sounds of nature – and specifically the dawn chorus – have a positive effect on human health and well-being. 'Ecotherapy' is now being recommended by doctors as an antidote to depression and anxiety, with time spent in the outdoors having an uplifting effect on mind and body.

Since the environmentalist and broadcaster Chris Baines held his birthday party at 4am at Moseley Bog in Birmingham in 1984, so that all of his guests could listen to the dawn chorus together, International Dawn Chorus Day has become a worldwide phenomenon celebrated in more than 80 countries. Organised by The Wildlife Trusts, it is held on the first Sunday in May. There are also many guided walks on offer led by experts up and down the country. Failing that, as long as you are literally 'up with the lark', listening at an open window may be all that is required for a front row seat at a world-class concert.

Golden Eagles

Lions of the Sky

The golden eagle has cast a spell over the human race since ancient times. Everyone from poets and artists to kings and emperors has sought to glorify or identify with its authority. The ruler of the raptors; the lion of the sky.

First there are the eyes: translucent, far-seeing, unflinching, and a frown that is enigmatic and impossible to interpret. Then there is its beak, sharp enough to slice through flesh like a razor, and the crown of golden feathers that adorns its head and neck. Framing all of this are dark wings punctuated with a band of white, like ermine draped around the cloak of a medieval monarch.

To watch a golden eagle take off from its mountain lair is to witness raw power unleashed. The head shoots forwards as its huge wings are unfurled. Enveloping its body, they can measure a full 7ft (over 2m) from wingtip to wingtip, ending in long finger-like feathers. Much mimicked by human flying machines, the eagle soars up on thermals with brief wingbeats, holding its wings in a shallow 'V' shape. When it dives, swooping out of the skies with deadly intent, it can reach speeds of up to 200mph (320km/h), before clamping those giant talons around its prey in a vice-like grip.

Shy and wary of humans, golden eagles favour mountains on which to build their eyries (nests), preferring cliff edges overlooking remote glens and wild open moorlands where they can more easily see their prey (rabbits, hares, grouse, ptarmigan and carrion). With eyesight eight times better than our own, they can spot a meal up to 2 miles (over 3km) away.

Golden eagles were widespread around the UK until the 1700s, when a purge by over-zealous sheep farmers and, later, Victorian gamekeepers saw the population plummet to around 100 pairs by the early 20th century. As Scotland's unofficial national bird, eagles have full protection in UK law (it is an offence to go near an eagle's nest at any time of year), and there are now around 500 pairs. Apart from a single pair in England, which were seen regularly near Haweswater in the Lake District until 2015, all golden eagles are found in Scotland, mainly in the highlands and islands. A notable exception has been Orkney, where breeding golden eagles declined to just one pair by the mid-19th century. There was a brief resurgence between 1966 and 1982, but no sightings after that until 2021, when RSPB Scotland reported golden eagles nesting at their nature reserve in Hoy. In addition, 2018 saw the launch of a project to reintroduce the species into the south of Scotland, and thousands of people have taken part in initiatives to help achieve this aim.

Within their range, golden eagles can be seen year-round, with early spring being particularly rewarding when they engage in territorial displays. The most reliable sightings are to be had on the Inner and Outer Hebrides, with Skye (Glen Brittle Forest), Raasay, Islay (Oa Peninsula), Mull (also known as Eagle Island), Rum and Harris (North Harris Eagle Observatory) blessed with some of the densest populations in Europe. In the Firth of Clyde, the Isle of Arran (around the village of Lochranza) has also had excellent sightings in recent years. On the mainland, the Northern Highlands, including the Findhorn Valley, the Cairngorms (Glenmore Forest Park) and Glen Affric, are all home to the lion of the sky.

Ospreys

Return of the Fisher King

The conservation of rare birds in Britain would be in a much poorer state without the efforts of Roy Dennis. A field ornithologist, wildlife consultant, author, lecturer and broadcaster, he founded a charitable trust dedicated to wildlife conservation and research in 1995, now called the Roy Dennis Wildlife Foundation. One of the raptors with which Dennis's name is most closely associated is the osprey. While ospreys are found throughout the world, and were once widespread in Britain, they were hunted to extinction in England in the 19th century and in Scotland in the early 20th century.

Happily, in the 1950s a breeding pair re-established themselves at RSPB Loch Garten Nature Reserve near Aviemore in the Scottish Highlands, where their descendants now receive more than 35,000 visitors a year. Fifty years later, Dennis helped to introduce ospreys to Rutland Water in the East Midlands; today more than 150 young birds have fledged from nests in the area since the first chick did so in 2001.

Ospreys are migratory birds that arrive in Britain in mid-March and return to Africa in October for the winter. Their heads are white, with piercing yellow eyes and a distinctive brown eyestripe. Dark above and lighter below, their wings can sometimes measure up to 6ft (1.8m) from wingtip to wingtip.

Like many birds of prey, ospreys are thrilling to watch in flight, particularly when they are hunting for their one and only source of food – fish. Their hunting flight involves circling in the skies above lakes, rivers and estuaries while concentrating intently on the waters below. Having spotted its prey, the osprey folds its wings into a distinctive 'W' shape and torpedoes towards the water, before thrusting its feet forwards at the last moment and crashing into the water with a dramatic splash.

The osprey's extraordinary speed, agility and focus is complemented with talons that are not only long, curved and as sharp as razors, but also have adhesive scales. Even though its tremendous wingbeat has evolved to give maximum lift, taking off from the water again can sometimes be an immense struggle, especially when carrying a fish as heavy as the osprey itself. There are tales of individuals being dragged down into the water, unable to detach themselves. If the hunt is successful, the osprey will return to land to enjoy its hard-won meal, holding its prey with the head facing forwards to reduce resistance from the wind.

Due to natural recolonisation and translocation projects, such as those of Roy Dennis and his team, osprey numbers have significantly increased in recent years – there are now an estimated 300 pairs breeding in mainland Britain. While most of these are in Scotland, breeding birds have also been recorded further south in Kielder Forest in Northumberland, the Lake District (with its famous pair on Bassenthwaite Lake near Keswick), Rutland Water Nature Reserve in the East Midlands and the Cors Dyfi Nature Reserve in Powys, near the west coast of Wales.

The most recent translocation project to Poole Harbour in Dorset will hopefully result in even more breeding pairs. If successful, it will be the first time ospreys have bred on the south coast of England for hundreds of years.

Red Kites

The Comeback Kid

Over the last thousand years, few species have endured such an extreme roller-coaster ride of royal protection, persecution, near elimination and popular revival as the red kite. Once revered as a saviour scavenger that helped clean the filthy streets of medieval England, it was later treated as vermin before being hunted to near extinction in Victorian times. From its last redoubt in Wales, where in the 1950s its numbers were reduced to 10 breeding pairs, this majestic raptor has recently made a remarkable comeback following its reintroduction to the Chilterns in 1990.

This RSPB-led project has been hailed as a great conservation success story. It was achieved after 13 young birds were brought over from Spain and

released into the area. This success was then replicated in northern and central Scotland, Yorkshire and Northamptonshire, with birds from Sweden and other parts of Europe. In 2008, kites were also reintroduced to the Mourne Mountains of Northern Ireland after a 170-year absence. Populations have established themselves quickly, particularly in southern England, and there are now an estimated 4,500 breeding pairs in the UK.

The red kite is one of the most graceful and athletic birds, a true acrobat of the sky. The wingspan of a fully grown adult can measure more than 5ft (1.5m). In flight, the wings are held well forwards at a slight angle with five long black feathers at the end of each wing. The combination of these vast wings and a body that weighs around 2.25lb (1kg) means that kites can hover in the air for several minutes at a time while barely moving.

The red kite's colouring is primarily chestnut brown (rufous), with a light-grey head and distinctive white markings on the underside of its wings. Its reddish-brown forked tail constantly swivels in flight like a rudder as it twists and turns in search of prey, with eyes constantly scanning the ground below. The bird's high-pitched whistling call is easy to recognise.

Kites like rolling country where they can catch the updrafts rising from the hills while patrolling the borders of woods and open fields. They feed primarily on carrion, which is why they are often seen hovering over motorways such as the M4 and the M40 on the look-out for roadkill, but their true grace is better appreciated in their more rural strongholds.

There are now some approved feeding stations and trails around the UK, offering an opportunity to watch kites flying and feeding. Gigrin Farm, near Rhayader in Wales, has five large hides as well as specialist shelters for photographers and film-makers. There is also a circular 11-mile (17.7-km) Red Kite Trail through a mix of mature woodland, wetland and open countryside in the lower Derwent Valley in County Durham, starting and finishing in Gateshead.

Kites can also be seen in beautiful rural scenery along the Galloway Kite Trail around Loch Ken in the south-west of Scotland. While at Argaty farm estate near Stirling in central Scotland, another small group of kites has recently been reintroduced. At the latter there is a feeding station with a purpose-built hide from which to view the birds.

Owls

A Little Night Music

We all know what they sound like, even if we rarely see them. For, in truth, few of nature's high-profile stars live so close to us and yet are seen so little. When we were young, many of us tried to imitate the hoot of an owl through our clasped hands and thumbs, in response to the call of one of these elusive creatures. But we would probably be unaware, both then and now, that a rough translation of the bird's apparently friendly retort was most likely to have been a robust 'Clear 'orf, mate. This is my patch, not yours!'

Five species of owl are commonly found in the UK: the barn owl, tawny owl, long-eared owl, short-eared owl and little owl. Of these, the barn owl and the tawny owl are the most familiar: the former with a snow-white,

heart-shaped face, light-brown wings and downy chest feathers; the latter, more rotund in appearance, with brown feathers around the face, large black eyes and mottled, reddish-brown wings.

In contrast to most birds, owls have eyes on the front rather than the sides of their heads, which, as well as giving them their wise appearance, provides excellent depth of vision when hunting. In order to see left and right, owls are able to rotate their necks up to 270 degrees in each direction.

The call of the tawny owl is probably the most imitated of all birds, characterised as the famous 'to-whit, to-woo', but in reality it is a sound more like a long, quavering 'whoo ... hooo' (male), or the less familiar 'kee ... wick' (female). What people think of as the call of a single bird is actually the sound of a pair of tawnys calling to one another. The screech of the barn owl could hardly be more different and is usually heard in spring when the males are calling for females to nest.

Tawny owls are most vocal in the autumn and winter when they are establishing territories, pairing off and later nesting. By this time, the offspring

of the previous breeding season have been turfed out of their nests, and this prime real estate, with all the hunting territory that goes with it, is fair game.

Night-time sightings of owls, while invariably atmospheric, are more often than not just a ghostly fly-by, caught in the glare of car headlights. You could stumble across a tawny owl's woodland roost site, or spot a short-eared or barn owl in winter as they patrol meadows and marshlands on the lookout for field voles that make up the majority of their diet. Making use of their highly sensitive hearing and superior sight, an owl's hunting or 'quartering' flight – flapping, gliding and hovering in search of a meal – ends with a sudden pounce onto its unsuspecting prey.

Owls are widespread throughout the UK, although populations of the different species vary regionally. Hotspots include large parts of East Anglia and the Somerset Levels, while RSPB Lakenheath Fen Reserve, a large wetland south of the Little Ouse in Suffolk, runs guided owl walks. At dawn and dusk in summer, barn owls can regularly be seen hunting for voles and mice at RSPB Ham Wall Reserve in the Avalon Marshes in Somerset.

Peregrine Falcons

The World's Fastest Animal

While the ongoing debate over the veracity of UFOs remains unsolved, it is sometimes tempting to think the solution might be hiding in plain sight. My vote goes to the peregrine falcon. Like any realistic contender, it is a miracle of aerodynamic design. Caught on camera while hunting, it can be seen torpedoing out of the sky in a manoeuvre called a 'stoop'. Sometimes diving from more than a mile (1.6km) high, the peregrine opens its wings in an 'M' shape just before it strikes, plucking its victim clean out of the air. Set against a featureless sky, its speed relative to its prey can sometimes look uncannily like much UFO footage.

This formidable aerial gymnast feeds almost exclusively on medium-sized birds such as pigeons and waterfowl, which it hunts on the wing, usually at dawn and dusk. Peregrines can spot their prey from nearly 2 miles (3.2km) away and have been recorded diving at speeds of 242mph (390km/h), making it the fastest animal on the planet.

It has a broad, powerful body with pointed wings that reduce drag in flight and fold back tightly against its body when flying in a stoop. The force of the air blowing into its lungs would be enough to burst them open, were it not for tiny bones in its nostrils that reduce the pressure – an innovation of evolution that has been borrowed by the designers of jet engines.

The peregrine is the largest British falcon, a family that includes the merlin, the hobby and the kestrel. Its head and back are slate-grey with a silky white chest and black bars on its lower body. Like other falcons, it has an extravagant black 'moustache' on its face that surrounds its snow-white chin feathers. It is also sexually dimorphic, with females often considerably larger than males.

While there are currently thought to be around 1,700 breeding pairs in Britain, peregrine numbers reached an all-time low in the 1950s and 60s when organochlorine-based insecticides used in gardens and agriculture entered its food chain. As well as poisoning the adults, the females also began to lay eggs with shells that were too thin to survive incubation. Since these pesticides have been banned in most of Europe, British populations have recovered to levels not seen for many centuries.

Peregrines can now be found nesting in the tall buildings of many cities around the country, including London, Bath, Derby, Exeter and Sheffield. One of its favoured nesting sites is in the spires of churches and cathedrals, primarily due to their height and panoramic views of the surrounding hunting grounds. Recent examples include the cathedrals at Salisbury, Norwich, Wakefield, Chichester and Ely. Although webcams have raised the profile of urban peregrines, city sites only account for around a hundred pairs. Most peregrines nest high up on cliffs around the British coastline, with other strongholds on the inland mountains of the north and west.

Anyone who wants to learn more about the peregrine falcon may enjoy one of the most critically acclaimed nature books of the last century, J. A. Baker's *The Peregrine* (1967). Written in diary form, it records the author's lyrical observations on the peregrines that nested near his home in Essex during the winter of 1962–3.

Nightingales

Vanishing Virtuosos

It is mid-May, just before midnight. I am walking in single file in complete silence along a disused railway line in East Sussex. It is pitch black and our small group is treading as lightly and delicately as it can with torches turned off. On a pre-arranged signal, we all shuffle to a halt. And wait. The sound of silence is deafening, punctuated only by the odd muffled cough or a stick breaking underfoot.

Suddenly, the soloist we have all come to hear breaks into song. This is birdsong as I've never heard it before. When a cellist starts playing and a human voice begins to sing, the nightingale responds in turn with a change of tune, rhythm and tempo. If this isn't a taste of the sublime, then what is?

Since 2014, folk singer Sam Lee has been taking small groups for an experience inspired by the BBC's first live broadcast on 19 May 1924, when legendary cellist, Beatrice Harrison, accompanied the song of a nightingale. Sam believes that spending time in nature with the nightingale can hold up a mirror to our own inner world. His award-winning book, *The Nightingale: Notes on a Songbird* (2021), is a passionate reimagining of the bird as a symbol of resistance to the environmental destruction of modern times.

Nightingales can produce more than 1,500 different sounds, and have a range of more than 250 musical phrases, which they use as a song of seduction to attract mates and proclaim their territory. Using words to describe or imitate birdsong is a bit like using mathematical equations to describe feelings, but here are a few attempts: liquid, fluting, trilling, chitter-chatter, 'tu-tu-tu'.

Slightly larger than robins, with plain brown plumage above and creamy-white below, nightingales are usually very difficult to see. Their preferred living quarters are located in the scrubby underworld of woods and forests, where they can nest protected from predators. In spite of its unassuming appearance, the nightingale has featured in mythology and literature throughout history and around the world as a symbol of death, sorrow, beauty and love, by writers such as Ovid, Chaucer, Shakespeare, Keats and Emily Dickinson.

Nightingales migrate from western Africa, arriving in mid-April, and staying until August. The peak of their singing season is between April and early June, keeping their sweetest arias for night-time between midnight and dawn, although they do sometimes sing during the day. Due to habitat loss both in their wintering grounds in Africa and the UK, and the rise of deer populations that damage their woodland nesting sites, over the last 40 years there has been a tragic 90 per cent decline in numbers in the UK.

Today the nightingale's breeding grounds have contracted almost entirely to the south-east of England, with the highest densities in Essex, Suffolk, Norfolk, Kent and Sussex. One notable success has been the increase in numbers on the Knepp Estate in West Sussex, famous for its rewilding story, which now has one of the highest concentrations of nightingales in Britain.

Kingfishers

Nature's Bullet Train

It is the vivid colouring of the kingfisher that sets it apart. Its back and wings are a stunning spectrum of metallic blues, while its orange claws and chest are topped by a white chin and the black spear of its bill. There are more than 100 species worldwide, but only the common kingfisher (*Alcedo atthis*) is found in Britain.

The combination of its size (similar to a house sparrow) and shape make it an expert diver that can penetrate the surface of a river at 25mph (40km/h). As well as its jet-fighter flight pattern, reaching speeds of up to 50mph (80km/h) as it flies low over the water, the secret to the kingfisher's lethal prowess is the streamlined shape of its long, pointed beak.

The kingfisher provided the inspiration for one of modern technology's most successful examples of biomimicry, a process whereby designers imitate the forms of nature evolved over millennia to solve the design challenges of today. In the 1990s, the nose of the Japanese Shinkansen bullet train was remodelled to create a superbly efficient aerodynamic shape based on the kingfisher's bill.

Kingfishers have specially adapted eyesight that allows them to switch to binocular vision under water. Their eyes adjust to the refraction of water while accurately judging the distance of their prey, and a special membrane protects their eyes and allows them to see in cloudy water. This combination of skills make them highly efficient hunters of minnows and sticklebacks, their primary diet, and they can catch more than 100 in a day.

Kingfishers are difficult to see – often just glimpsed as a flash of brilliant blue – as they are shy and solitary birds. They prefer slow-moving river or lake environments, where the banks are surrounded by reeds or trees, with low-hanging branches such as willows and alders. They are also territorial

around their feeding range, but will look for a mate in early spring, building their burrows in sandy river banks. The females lay up to three clutches of around six or seven eggs in a season.

Kingfishers have long been associated with folklore and mythology. In ancient Greece, it was identified with the mythical 'halcyon' bird, which made its nest from a raft of fish bones while floating at sea and was able to calm the winds and the waves, giving rise to the expression 'halcyon days'. Other traditions associate the kingfisher with Noah, who sent what was previously a drab grey bird on a reconnaissance mission from his Ark; as a consequence the kingfisher gained its bright colours from the sky and the sun as it reappeared after the deluge.

The kingfisher is more commonly seen in the south of Britain than the north, but numbers are now reported to be increasing in Scotland. Rye Meads in Hertfordshire (RSPB), the London Wetland Centre (WWT), Lackford Lakes Nature Reserve in Suffolk and Staveley Nature Reserve in Yorkshire (Wildlife Trusts) are all excellent viewing sites.

Seabird Cities

Coastal Cacophonies

Seabirds need coastlines. Although many spend much of their lives over the sea, they still need terra firma to lay their eggs and raise their young in the spring and summer. The result is a wildlife extravaganza in some of the most remote and beautiful locations in Britain.

SCOTLAND

St Abb's Head, Eyemouth
Located on the east coast of Scotland just north of the border, St Abbs is home to tens of thousands of guillemots (its star attraction), kittiwakes, razorbills, shags, herring gulls and fulmars. Known for its vertical cliffs and offshore stacks, it is one of Britain's most accessible seabird sites, with some spectacular viewing points.

Bass Rock, Firth of Forth
From late January, more than 70,000 pairs of gannets, the northern hemisphere's largest colony, return to this tiny volcanic plug of rock covering little more than 7 acres (2.8ha) in the waters of the Firth of Forth. The seabird population expands to around half a million in the spring and summer, when puffins, kittiwakes, guillemots, razorbills, fulmars and shags join the party. The Scottish Seabird Centre in adjacent North Berwick runs cruises around the island.

Hermaness, Shetland Islands
Located on the island of Unst, Hermaness lies at Britain's most northerly tip.

Its sheer cliffs – some of them almost 600ft (183m) high – are populated with gannets, guillemots, razorbills, fulmars, kittiwakes and shags. It is also one of the best locations in Britain to get close to puffins nesting in their burrows at the top of the cliffs. But beware great skuas known as 'bonxies', which are notorious for dive-bombing unwary visitors.

St Kilda, Outer Hebrides
The spectacular cliffs of this remote archipelago in the far west of the Hebrides are home to an estimated one million seabirds, Britain's largest colony of both fulmars and puffins, as well as shearwater, petrel, kittiwake and shags. It also boasts a colony of tens of thousands of Leach's petrel, 90 per cent of the European breeding population.

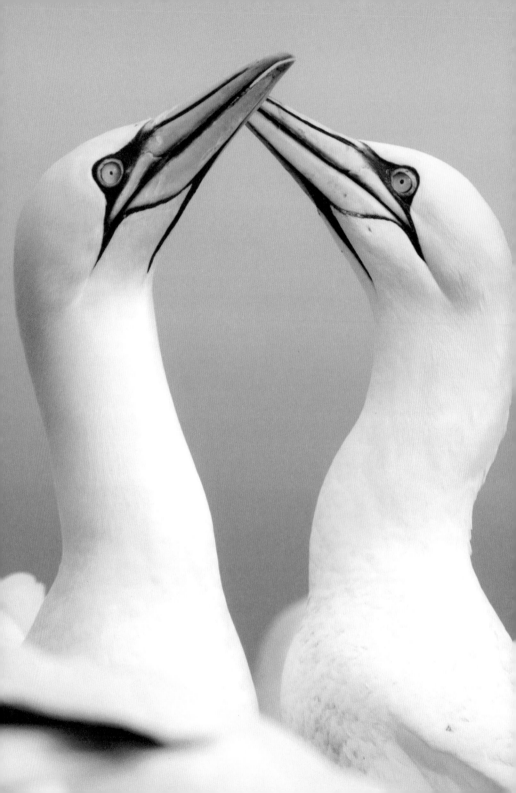

ENGLAND

Bempton Cliffs and Flamborough Head, Yorkshire

During the spring and summer, Bempton Cliffs Nature Reserve on the Yorkshire coast is home to another of the UK's top wildlife spectacles. Around half a million seabirds gather here, including guillemots, gannets, razorbills and puffins. A few miles south, the beaches and 400ft (122m) chalk cliffs of Flamborough Head are home to oystercatchers, gulls and cormorants.

Farne Islands, Northumberland

Sir David Attenborough's favourite British wildlife site offers close encounters with large populations of Arctic terns, kittiwakes, razorbills, eider ducks and guillemots. The Farne Islands are also among the best places to see one of the nation's favourite birds, the puffin, with around 43,000 breeding pairs.

WALES

Skomer Island, St Bride's Bay, Pembrokeshire

The most important seabird site in southern Britain, Skomer is home to fulmars, kittiwakes, guillemots, gannets and puffins among many other seabirds. Along with its sister islands Skokholm and Middleholm, the archipelago also hosts an estimated 100,000 pairs of nesting Manx shearwaters, about 40 per cent of the total world population.

South Stack Cliffs, Holy Island, Anglesey

Off the western side of Anglesey, Holy Island is made up of heathland and farmland surrounded by a stretch of dramatic sea cliffs that look out over the islets of South Stack to the north-west. In spring, Ellin's Tower provides excellent views of guillemots, razorbills, puffins, kittiwakes, fulmars and gulls on the cliff ledges.

Skylarks

Our National Songbird

No other bird captures the essence of summer like the skylark. Its song has long been associated with the divine, not just because of its energy and complexity, but also because it often sings out of sight, flying so high it can barely be seen. It has inspired poets and composers from Percy Bysshe Shelley to Vaughan Williams, with the latter's work 'The Lark Ascending' regularly voted Britain's favourite piece of music.

Like all songbirds, the male skylark sings to protect its territory and attract a mate. The sheer gusto with which it performs is a signal to any competing male or receptive female that it is the healthiest, strongest individual around with the best genes to pass on to the next generation. In the countryside, it is among the first birds to announce the break of day, singing to an audience that is 'up with the lark'.

As well as its high-speed trilling motifs at the top of the treble register, the skylark's song is remarkable for its unbroken trajectory, sometimes continuing without a break for up to five minutes at a time, and often performed during its steepling ascent into the sky, occasionally as high as 1,000ft (over 300m) above the ground, followed by an effortless hover and a slow, spiralling descent.

Skylarks are with us throughout the year; they may even sing on sunny days in late winter and go on until late summer. One reason why the song of the skylark is still identified with summer is its preference for open areas of farm and grassland. For all those who worked the land before the Industrial Revolution, this ecstatic sound would have been as familiar as a radio playing music in the background is today, an experience that has been passed down in the collective memory.

Like the nightingale, the skylark's legendary voice is contradicted by its prosaic appearance. Small and stocky with streaky brown feathers and off-white underparts, skylarks are a classic example of the proverbial LBJ (little brown job) of birding parlance, but one with the voice of an opera star. Its only concession to celebrity status is the punk-style crest on its head, which it usually only deploys when frightened or alarmed.

For such an ethereal bird, it may come as a surprise to learn that skylarks nest and feed almost exclusively on the ground. Sadly, its fondness for open, arable fields is likely the reason behind its steep decline: skylark numbers have dropped by more than 60 per cent since 1970. Intensive farming practices are thought to be to blame. These include the increased use of pesticides and the planting of crops year-round that deny the skylarks their winter food source of left-over seeds following the autumn harvest.

Some farmers are taking note, however, and leaving small patches ('skylark plots') left unsown in fields with winter cereals, which increases nesting opportunities and food availability. On a number of areas of farmland owned by the National Trust, including around the White Cliffs of Dover and sites in Pembrokeshire, changes in farming practices have already led to an increase in skylark numbers.

Avian Migrations

Birds of a Feather

To the non-birder, it all seems obvious. The temperature cools, the nights draw in and just as humans begin to retreat inside their houses, so too migrating birds fly south for the winter. In spring, everything happens in reverse. As the leaves return to the trees and the air begins to warm, so the same birds come flocking back. The reality, as with many of nature's annual rituals, is a little more complex.

Many of Britain's bird species migrate. Several of them are insect-eaters such as swifts, swallows, nightingales and cuckoos, which can find more food by heading south during the winter months. Meanwhile, others arrive

from the continent to spend the winter here. These include a variety of geese, swans, ducks and waders. One bird's empty larder, it seems, is another's sumptuous feast.

To complicate matters further, there are still other birds known as 'passage migrants', which use our islands as a refuelling stop on their way back and forth from the Arctic, Scandinavia, Eastern Europe and Russia. These species include little gulls, black tern and wryneck. Finally, there are the 'partial migrants', birds of the same species that choose different strategies depending on where they have spent the breeding season, and include many common birds such as robins, starlings, goldfinches and lapwings.

Whichever group they fall into, migrating birds always rank high in the calendar of wildlife events. The only question is where to find the best places to see them in the largest numbers as they depart or arrive. Coastal headlands, promontories, capes, points, cliffs, bluffs and any other sections of coast that jut out into the sea are certainly not bad places to start. Whether arriving in April or May, or departing in September or October, many of these first and last signatures of land become like avian passenger terminals thronging with activity.

Top of the list is Spurn Point, a narrow 3-mile (4.8-km) long spit of sand and shingle jutting out across the mouth of the River Humber in Yorkshire, where it flows into the North Sea. It is estimated that up to 15,000 birds pass the Bird Observatory on a busy morning in autumn. Alongside its regular inhabitants of seabirds and waders, large 'falls' of small migrating birds such as thrushes, pipits, goldcrests, whinchats and redstarts are a good bet, with an outside chance of seeing off-course rarities such as the black-browed albatross that was recorded in 2002. So famous is Spurn for its migratory birds that a Migration Festival is usually held every September.

Other migration hotspots include the 400ft (122m) chalk cliffs at Flamborough Head, also on the Yorkshire coast, where thousands of wheatears, willow warblers and wagtails can be seen in autumn. An onshore breeze from the east, blowing migrants over the North Sea when there is poor visibility out to sea, will often encourage them to land at the first opportunity. In the south of England, other high-volume sites include Snettisham RSPB Nature Reserve on the Norfolk coast (wintering Arctic wildfowl), Beachy Head in East Sussex, the Isle of Portland in Dorset and the Isles of Scilly off Land's End in Cornwall.

Avocets

Conservation Pin-up Stars

It wasn't just our valiant troops who arrived home triumphant on British shores at the end of the Second World War. In their wake came a bird that had been absent for at least a hundred years. The avocet, a striking wader with black-and-white plumage, stilt-like, grey-blue legs and trademark long upturned beak had not bred in the UK since the 1840s. The avocet's enemy had been homegrown in the form of the egg-collectors and hunters of Victorian Britain.

Its salvation came when a decision was made early on in the war to allow the coastal marshes of East Anglia to flood, making an attack from

German-occupied Holland much more difficult. In this case, the law of
unintended consequences paid rich dividends by turning the shores of Suffolk
into marshland, the perfect habitat for avocets.

The home they chose was Havergate Island, a 2-mile (3.2-km) strip of mud
and marsh in the estuary of the River Ore, protected from the North Sea by the
adjacent shingle spit of Orford Ness. Shortly afterwards, avocets also began to
breed in the Minsmere coastal wetlands to the north, an area that became an
RSPB reserve in 1947 and is now one of its flagship sites. To mark the success
of the avocet conservation project, the RSPB adopted the bird as its logo in
1955, and it remains one of the great conservation stories of the 20th century.
Each year from March onwards, the Scrape at Minsmere, an area of shallow
lagoons adjacent to the sea, teems with these elegant birds.

Avocets are among the most fascinating wading birds to watch. Like ducks,
they will sometimes upend themselves in deeper water while searching for
food. In the shallows, meanwhile, they can be seen sweeping their slightly
open, upturned bills from side to side sieving the sediment for tiny worms,
small insects and invertebrates. Their mating ritual is a fascinating dance as

the female holds her long neck down close to the water while her male suitor preens himself with his bill and splashes around her.

Since the 1970s, avocet numbers have increased along the east coast of England and now breed as far north as Humberside. In late summer, they can be seen taking part in the 'whirling wader spectacle' at Snettisham on the Wash in Norfolk, another RSPB reserve where tens of thousands of birds take flight as some of the highest tides of the year push them off the mudflats. They are also a year-round resident at Leighton Moss RSPB reserve on the north-west coast, alongside a wide range of spectacular wildlife, including otters, bearded tits, marsh harriers, egrets and red deer.

Migrating avocets can also be found during the winter months along the south coast and in the west of Britain. Poole Harbour in Dorset, location of the National Trust's Brownsea Island, is the most important wintering site for avocets in the UK. Around 2,000 birds arrive every autumn, including some from the Netherlands, an 80-fold increase over 30 years. RSPB avocet cruises also run along the Exe Estuary from Topsham in Devon, where the boats are able to get up close to flocks of these truly iconic birds.

Goldfinches

A Charm Offensive

The goldfinch's scarlet face, black-and-white head, light-brown body and brilliant yellow bar across the middle of its black wings make it hard to confuse with other garden favourites, such as chaffinches, blue tits or great tits. In bright sunlight, its wing beats create an unmistakable yellow blur.

Its song is one of the great pleasures of the British summer, performed at break-neck tempo with a babbling fluidity – a medley of notes of apparently infinite variety. Goldfinches frequently fly in flocks, singing in unison as they go. This is thought to be the origin of one of the most delightful collective nouns, a 'charm' of goldfinches, derived from the Old English word 'cirm', meaning 'chatter'.

Goldfinches feed primarily on the seeds of plants. Its narrow, pointed beak has ridges on the inside, which are perfectly adapted to the complicated process of extracting and eating the seeds of thorny plants, such as thistles and the brown oval heads of teasels. Its favourite are the tiny black seeds from the *Guizotia* flower (a relative of the sunflower) known as nyjer or niger. Nyjer seed is now frequently added to bird food and has contributed to the goldfinch becoming a much more common sight in our gardens. There are now thought to be around 1.2 million breeding pairs across Britain every summer, twice as many as in the 1970s.

Goldfinches are found throughout the British Isles, except for the very northern, mountainous areas of Scotland. They favour habitats with open areas of scattered trees and bushes, including open woodland, heaths, moors and farmland, as well as the parks and gardens of our towns and cities. Flocks often roost together in the branches of trees, particularly oak and beech, several miles from their feeding grounds. Due to their bone-dry diet they also need a good water source, and particularly enjoy bird baths, which provide hours of entertainment for both observer and observed during the summer months.

As a partial migrant, many goldfinches leave British shores for the winter – the speed with which their numbers contract depends largely on the severity of the autumn weather. Studies suggest that the females are more likely to migrate south, while the males that remain have the advantage of the best feeding and breeding territories come the spring.

Myth and folklore symbolically connect the goldfinch's red face and liking for thorny plants with the soul, death and resurrection. One legend tells of a goldfinch that took pity on Jesus and tried to remove his crown of thorns as he was carrying his cross to Golgotha. As it did so, a drop of blood dripped from Christ's head, giving the goldfinch its bright red face.

In the Victorian age, goldfinches became hugely popular as caged birds, due to a combination of their striking looks and captivating song, but their trapping caused the wild population to plummet. Halting this practice was one of the first successes of the Society for the Protection of Birds, which was founded in 1889 by Emily Williamson and later became the RSPB.

Swifts and Swallows

Nomads of the Sky

Of all the markers of the passing seasons, from bluebells in spring to conkers in autumn, few pluck at the heart strings more than the arrival and departure of swifts and swallows. These aerial nomads cover thousands of miles every year, flying back and forth between their breeding sites in the UK and their wintering grounds in sub-Saharan Africa.

In 2016, scientists were finally able to confirm something that had long been suspected – that most swifts never land during their epic flights south in autumn, remaining airborne for an incredible 10 months at a time. Feeding on insects, sleeping and even mating on the wing, swifts only land when they arrive back at their nesting sites in Europe the following spring.

It is even thought that, as young birds, swifts may remain in flight for as long as three years from first leaving the nest to returning as adults to lay their own eggs. Anders Hedenström, a professor at the University of Lund in Sweden who led the study, has calculated that the distance a swift can fly over a lifetime of 20 years is the same as travelling to the Moon and back seven times.

Swifts and swallows look similar in flight, as they both have forked tails. However, swifts are larger, fly higher and call more loudly. Its sooty brown feathers often appear dark grey against the sky and its boomerang profile makes it one of nature's most easily recognised and aerodynamic creations. Swallows, on other hand, are more brightly coloured with a glossy, steel-blue head and back, a red chin and snowy-white underparts. Their forked tail feathers, known as streamers, are also considerably longer.

Swallows arrive in the UK from the end of March, a month ahead of the swifts, which appear from the end of April or early May. Swifts then depart in the first week of August, while swallows remain until September or early October. When they arrive in the spring, after a six-week journey of more than 6,000 miles (9,650km) from their wintering sites in South Africa, swallows often return to the same nests they left the previous autumn. Their arrival is marked by a cacophony of twittering, which to an impartial observer sounds euphoric – most of us would probably feel the same if we had survived such an epic journey. In truth, it is all about re-establishing their territories for the upcoming nesting season.

Swifts are more than happy to nest in an urban environment. Their main priority is height and security. As the ultimate creature of the air, land-based take-offs are a serious challenge for the swift, having tiny feet relative to the size of their bodies. Their favoured nesting spots are in the eaves of old buildings, a behaviour that evolved from their original sites in the crevices of trees, caves and cliffs.

Sadly, due to changes in the way modern houses are built, suitable nesting locations are declining. An alternative option is to provide nesting boxes or 'swift bricks' – hollow bricks that can be built high up in the walls of new houses. The RSPB and Swift Conservation are working with housing developers and local councils around the UK to install these bricks in new buildings, hoping to reverse the fall in the numbers of such an iconic bird.

White-tailed Eagles

The Flying Barn Door

The white-tailed eagle has earned its moniker for a reason. Anyone who has ever witnessed the awe-inspiring sight of this magnificent creature swooping down over the seas surrounding the Isle of Mull to pluck a fish from the waves will know that the term 'flying barn door' is no exaggeration. It might also be known as the 'flying holy grail', so prized is it as a sighting among naturalists. With a wingspan of up to 8ft (2.4m), it is Britain's largest bird of prey.

As a student, long before I was lucky enough to see one in the wild, I had always associated eagles with a famous pub in Oxford called The Eagle and Child. This was the local haunt of the Inklings, a literary group whose members included J.R.R. Tolkien and C.S. Lewis. The pub's name apparently derives from a nobleman's crest, which in turn reflects a tradition that eagles are responsible for kidnapping babies.

Fostered perhaps by the Victorian gamekeepers whose job it was to eradicate raptors from their estates, this outdated belief can still be traced in the response to the recent reintroduction of white-tailed eagles to Fife in mainland Scotland. Happily they have proved to be a financial godsend. In 1975, 82 young birds from Norway were reintroduced to the island of Rhum, and 10 years later the first successful breeding in modern times took place on Mull. It is now estimated that white-tailed eagles bring in up to £5 million per year from eagle-related tourism. Nearby Skye is also a major beneficiary.

White-tailed eagles became extinct in England in the 19th century. The last breeding pair was recorded in 1916 on the Isle of Skye, before the last individual was killed in the Shetlands two years later. Today, however, reintroductions include the Isle of Wight (Ron Dennis Wildlife Foundation and Forestry England) with a licence granted for further reintroductions at Wild Ken Hill, a rewilding, conservation and sustainable farming project on the West Norfolk coast. The RSPB predict that by 2025 there could be as many as 200 breeding pairs around the UK.

Unless they are very close, identifying eagles can sometimes be difficult. The easiest mistake is to confuse them with buzzards, which are sometimes known by locals as 'tourist eagles'. White-tailed eagles are twice the size of buzzards, but when they are high in the sky with no reference point, it is best to look for the 'finger' feathers at the end of their wings; with buzzards, these are much shorter and closer together and sometimes can't even be seen at all.

Distinguishing white-tailed from golden eagles can also be a challenge, especially in places such as the Isle of Skye where they are often seen together. The former will usually have longer, wider wings and a more rectangular shape in line with their 'barn door' nickname. Their head and tail size are also different, with white-tailed eagles having a large head and smaller tail, while golden eagles have a smaller head and longer tail.

Herons

Greys, Egrets and Booming Bitterns

It is perhaps surprising that a world-class camouflage artist should want to advertise its presence with a loud booming voice, but the bittern is just such a creature. Renowned for being almost impossible to spot in a reedbed, its brown feathers are mottled with repeating patterns of dark brown stripes and flecks. When disturbed it freezes, pointing its bill at the sky, merging into its surroundings so well that it often seems to vanish entirely.

Come spring, however, its cloak of invisibility is penetrated by one of nature's most distinctive mating calls. Variously described as 'booming', 'bellowing', 'bumping', 'like a fog-horn' or 'air being blown over the lip of a bottle', it was once thought that the bittern produced its trademark call by immersing its beak in the water to amplify the sound. More recently, it has been discovered that the sound is produced by air being expelled from the powerful muscles surrounding the gullet. Rather than a visual count, which often proves impossible, its call is how the RSPB identifies the numbers of males on its reserves.

The booming bittern – once a prized dish at medieval banquets – has had a precarious history in the UK. By the 1870s it was considered extinct as a breeding species. It bred again in the early 20th century, but while numbers increased to around 80 breeding males in the 1950s, by the 1990s numbers had declined to fewer than 15. Thanks to concerted conservation efforts around the country, there are now thought to be around 200 permanent residents. Numbers can grow to around 600 in the winter, when an influx of visitors from colder nations swell our native population. One factor in the recovery of the bittern has been the successful development of reed management techniques in RSPB reserves such as Minsmere in Suffolk.

RSPB Leighton Moss in Lancashire is home to the largest reedbed in northern England and is another bittern stronghold. Wintering bitterns can also been seen at the WWT London Wetland Centre, where reedbeds and marshy grasslands have replaced four old reservoirs in the south-west of the city.

Much easier to spot are the bittern's more visible cousins, the grey heron and the egrets (cattle, great white and little egret). From February, grey herons can be seen at their nesting sites (heronries), which can be found throughout the UK. These heronries sometimes house up to 40 nesting pairs, busy repairing their nests from the previous year and preparing to lay their new clutch of eggs. During the nesting season, there is also a good chance of seeing a heron in flight, with its harpoon-like, pinkish-orange beak, jaunty plume of black feathers on the back of its head, 'S'-shaped neck and huge wings with a span of up to 6ft (1.8m). The ancient oaks of Swell Wood on the Somerset Levels are home to 100 pairs of nesting herons, the largest colony in south-west England.

The little egret, our smallest heron, with its white plumes, black legs and yellow feet, is widespread in England, Wales and Ireland, and is pushing north into Scotland. The great white egret, equivalent in size to the grey heron, has colonised Britain from its strongholds in mainland Europe.

Pink-footed Geese

'V' is for ... *Anser brachyrhynchus*

The annual return of migratory pink-footed geese to British shores is always a cause for celebration. With them comes not just the life-affirming cacophony of hundreds of these high-pitched honking, gabbling, gobbling and (surely) gossiping creatures flying overhead, but also the glorious sight of the 'V' formations in which they fly. Their flocks often number several thousand individuals, in contrast to other species, such as the Brent goose, which flock in their hundreds.

As its common name suggests, the most distinctive features of *Anser brachyrhynchus* are its pink legs and feet. Smaller than a mute swan, but bigger than a mallard, it is a medium-sized goose with a relatively short neck, rounded head and short beak. Its colouring is predominantly light brown with a dark brown head, light undertail and barred wings.

The reason for its 'V'-shaped flocking pattern, also known as a skein, may simply be a case of 'follow my leader'. However, scientific studies have shown that long-winged birds such as geese fly behind and slightly to the side of the bird in front in order to catch rising columns of air. This is nowhere near as easy as running or cycling in someone else's slipstream as humans do, because the birds need to find an aerodynamic sweet spot, timing their wing beats precisely to catch the climbing draughts and avoid those pulling them downwards.

Pink-footed geese spend their summers at Arctic latitudes in Iceland, Svalbard and Greenland. Here they breed before escaping the freezing clutches of the Arctic winter, reaching Scotland in October, where many of them stay, and Norfolk in November, where around 100,000 spend the winter. They roost around the Wash and the North Norfolk coast, nesting on estuaries or large bodies of fresh water, mudflats, moorland pools and floodwater, before departing again in April.

The daily routine of the pink-footed geese during their sojourn in Norfolk involves flying inland to the fields further west to feed on the rich pickings of the remnants of the annual harvest. This includes grain and root crops such as sugar beet and potatoes, which they use to supplement their diet of invertebrates from the coastal marshlands. The best time to watch them is at dawn or dusk as they commute between their roosting and feeding sites when the low winter light often transforms the landscape into an artist's palette, making the scene even more atmospheric.

The best places in Norfolk to see pink-footed geese are Blakeney Freshes in the marshes behind the spit at Blakeney Point, where the National Trust carries out bird counts every year to monitor numbers; RSPB Snettisham in West Norfolk; and Holkham, England's largest National Nature Reserve. In Scotland, top sites include Montrose Basin, Angus, where the tidal estuary of the River South Esk has created an area of wetlands roughly 2 miles (3.2km) square for the geese to roost and feed, and Aberlady Bay in the Firth of Forth near Edinburgh.

TREES
FLOWERS
& FUNGI

Bluebell Woods

Spring's Magic Carpet

Nothing represents the promise of renewal and hope more than a deep blue lake of bluebells on the floor of an ancient forest, lit by shafts of early morning sunlight. For lovers of the British countryside, this intoxicating sight, accompanied by the glorious sound of the dawn chorus, is heaven indeed.

It is hardly surprising, then, that folklore and fairy magic have surrounded bluebells throughout history, with countless tales of their effects on suggestible humans. They are associated with truth and humility and were once used in love spells to win over a loved one, or even to keep nightmares at bay when kept in a pillow or near the bed.

According to the Woodland Trust, up to half of the world's bluebells grow in the UK, and most of the rest are to be found in Western Europe. They seem to thrive where the climate is mild. We may be envious of places with scorching summers or white Christmases, but the UK's less extreme weather is just what bluebells need.

Our native bluebell (*Hyacinthoides non-scripta*) is an indicator species – along with plants such as lily of the valley, wood anemone, wild garlic and primrose – that the surrounding forest may be ancient woodland. This is defined as an area that has had continuous tree cover since 1600 in England and Wales, and 1750 in Scotland. Now reduced to just 2.5 per cent of the land in the UK, ancient woodland is remarkable for its biodiversity – each area unique and irreplaceable – and another reason to revere our ancient bluebell woods.

But don't be fooled. The apparent fecundity of bluebells can sometimes blind us to their sensitivity. They take many decades to grow and an individual seed takes at least five years to become a bulb and produce a flower. They also

take years to recover, if they do at all, when their leaves are crushed by walkers, as they are no longer able to photosynthesise.

Another threat to their existence is the rise of the Spanish bluebell (*Hyacinthoides hispanica*) – a variety that has proved popular with gardeners after being introduced in the 1600s. It rapidly forms a hybrid variety with the wild bluebell when it escapes onto roadside verges and into neighbouring woodland. Telling the difference between the two is quite easy when you know how, as the flowers of the Spanish bluebell are larger, more erect and lighter in colour. Their leaves are also thicker.

There are many bluebell woods cared for by the National Trust, including Emmetts Garden in Kent, Sheffield Park and Garden in East Sussex, the Blickling Estate in Norfolk (where Anne Boleyn was born) and Plas yn Rhiw overlooking Cardigan Bay in Wales. A more unusual but equally dramatic display can be seen on Skomer Island off the west coast of Pembrokeshire where, each year, bluebells carpet the foreshore with not a tree in sight.

Ancient Trees

Eyewitnesses to History

Trees are among the world's oldest living organisms. Human lifespans don't even come close. If you play under a 600-year-old oak as a child, there is every chance that it will still be growing long after you are gone. There is no set age at which a tree is classified as 'ancient', as trees age at different speeds. However, there are certain characteristics that mark them out as arboreal veterans.

One of the most vivid descriptions is that of Reverend Francis Kilvert, who wrote in his diary in 1876 of some local oak trees in Herefordshire: 'I fear those grey old men of Moccas Park, those grey, gnarled, low-browed, knock-kneed, bowed, bent, huge, strange, long-armed, deformed, hunched-backed, misshapen oak men that stand waiting and watching century after century.'

As the years pass, the trunks of long-lived species, such as oak, yew, ash, sweet chestnut and beech, grow wider and hollow out as the crown of the tree becomes smaller. Most distinctive of all are the incredible shapes that result from the weird contortions of roots, trunks and branches as the ever-changing weather and surrounding environment evolves over time.

The older a tree gets, the more diverse its ecology becomes. The deep fissures of its bark and the curves of its roots become important habitats for the species that depend on it, forming a biodiversity hotspot of fungi, decaying wood, invertebrates and lichen that in turn supports the surrounding ecosystem.

The National Trust looks after many of the oldest and most historically important trees in Britain and ensures they are being managed for the greatest possible longevity. These include the Ankerwycke Yew near Runnymede in Surrey, the Stonehenge of the arboreal world, which is thought to be around 2,500 years old. It is a possible site for the sealing of the Magna Carta in 1215, as well as early trysts between Henry VIII and Anne Boleyn.

Another of the Trust's notable trees is the apple tree at Woolsthorpe Manor, which inspired Sir Isaac Newton's law of gravity. Growing in the orchard of the Lincolnshire farmhouse, where Newton was born and later lived during the 1665 plague, the tree is now part of scientific legend. Yet there is a core of truth to the story, which an ageing Newton told to his friends William Stukeley and John Conduitt before he died. Seedlings from the tree now grow all over the world.

Wildflower Meadows

Flower Power

Downy-fruited sedge, meadow saffron, adder's-tongue fern, twayblade, ragged robin, mouse-ear hawkweed, fairy flax: even the names of our native wild flowers can strum the heart strings. Combine these Jackson Pollock-like splashes of colour with the heady scent of a hay meadow in high summer before the July harvest, and true paradise beckons.

Wildflower meadows were once widespread across lowland Britain, but due to intensive farming they have now almost entirely vanished from our countryside. Hundreds of thousands of acres of hay meadows have been ploughed up, and more than half the UK's hedgerows removed to create larger fields. Each year these were sprayed with pesticides, and those fields that

were returned to hay meadow were planted with quick-growing grasses that produced several harvests a year, as opposed to just one.

Nonetheless, there are signs that a revival is in the making, with gardeners leaving their lawns to flower, while farmers and conservationists restore colour to our grasslands. Not only are wildflower meadows a banquet for the senses, they also encourage biodiversity and support pollinating insects, which are vital for the health of our own food crops.

Any ancient wildflower meadows that have survived are few and far between. They are often found in places where intensive farming was more difficult, such as pasture alongside rivers that was hard to drain, and areas with less nutrient pollution. Wild flowers can easily be smothered by fast-growing grasses, brambles and thistles in soils that have been treated with fertilisers. Iffley Meadows outside Oxford is a fine example of an ancient wildflower meadow. Many of these pockets of farmland, which have only been farmed using traditional methods, are now owned and managed by conservation charities including the National Trust.

Another inspiring example of a traditional wildflower meadow is Clattinger Farm Nature Reserve, a 150 acre (61ha) lowland hay meadow in the Thames

floodplain, owned by the Wiltshire Wildlife Trust. A Site of Special Scientific Interest (SSSI), Clattinger is one of the few lowland farms in Britain to have never used artificial fertilisers to promote grass growth, which means that a diverse palette of wildflower species has been preserved. The result is a profusion of colour in spring and early summer. Stars of the show include snake's-head fritillaries, which appear in late April with their chequered purple and pink flowers – looking as much like designer lampshades as the snakeskin they are said to resemble. In August, there is meadow saffron (a pink flower, also known as autumn crocus) and tubular water-dropwort (white and pale pink), together with a huge range of orchids, including common spotted, heath spotted, southern marsh, burnt-tip and green-winged.

Many of the UK's finest remaining ancient wildflower meadows can be found in Devon and Cornwall, where species-rich culm grasslands with thick clay soils support a wide range of wild flowers. In Northern Ireland, the world-famous gardens and pleasure grounds at Mount Stewart are surrounded by wildflower meadows, in particular those of Ploughman's Hill and White Stag Mount found around the lake walk.

Heather Moorlands

Purple Haze

A deep swathe of colour has a powerful emotional impact in any landscape. Often it seems to symbolise an entire season: bluebells carpeting the floor of a forest in spring, for instance, or the bright orange leaves of a beech forest in autumn. In late summer, the sight of a heathland ablaze with purple heather inspires a similar response.

Although our heathlands often suggest untouched wilderness, they were almost invariably created by our prehistoric ancestors clearing forests during Bronze Age Britain, between 2500 and 800 BC, first to make spaces for hunting and later to graze livestock and grow crops. In later millennia, they became synonymous with the livelihoods of the rural poor, who used them for many

purposes, including fuel, food (honey produced by bees feeding on nectar from heathland plants), building materials (thatch), packing materials and rope.

As heather provides a sheltered environment for many species, it plays a key role in conserving biodiversity. It grows well in infertile acidic soils where it attracts nectar-loving insects such as butterflies and bees. It also provides a healthy habitat for reptiles, including lizards, adders and slow worms, as well as ground-nesting birds, including stonechats, wood larks and nightjars.

To the untrained eye, all heather looks pretty much the same, but there are in fact three main species and some rarer family members. Ling (*Calluna vulgaris*), bell heather (*Erica cinerea*) and cross-leaved heather (*E. tetralix*) are the most common varieties. Unlike bell and cross-leaved heather, the flowers of ling heather do not have a bell-shape, but are tightly packed towards the top of the stem, opening out like miniature tulips. Sometimes the flower of the ling grows white, as it does occasionally in Scotland and on Dartmoor, where local folklore holds that it will bring good luck.

Despite being a hardy species, heather requires careful management to thrive. At Dunwich Heath, the National Trust cuts the heather on rotation, so that the whole heathland won't suddenly reach the end of its life at the same time. Unwanted vegetation like bracken, gorse or scrub is also cut down and the ground scraped to expose the seeds, which can lie dormant for up to 60 years.

So familiar are we with the heather moorlands of the Scottish Highlands, which contain around 5 million acres (over 2 million hectares), it may come as a surprise that on a worldwide scale heather-dominated heathland is a relatively rare habitat.

Outside Scotland, upland heaths can be found in hilly areas of South West England, such as Dartmoor and Exmoor, central Wales and the Pennines. Lowland heath locations include the New Forest in Hampshire; the Lizard Peninsula in Cornwall – with its rare heather known as Cornish heath (*Erica vagans*); Dunwich Heath in Suffolk; and the area surrounding Poole in Dorset on the south coast, home to another rare heather, Dorset heath (*E. ciliaris*).

Autumn Leaves

Nature's Goodnight Kiss

The harvest has been brought in, thanks have been offered up to the Earth Goddess and the Green Man, and John Barleycorn is going to ground once more. Suddenly there are morning mists, and the nights are beginning to draw in. Although the fruit is heavy on the trees, and the hedgerows are alive with berries, there's an unmistakable chill in the air. There is the smell of bonfires and the crackle of beech and hazel nuts underfoot. Summer has departed.

But what a send-off this is. If anyone knows how to throw a farewell party, it's Mother Nature herself. 'So, you thought I only did green,' the message seems to be. 'Well how about this? Yellow, gold, orange, red, scarlet, purple, anyone? Try me and I will surpass your wildest imaginings.'

But why do the leaves change colour? What makes a maple leaf turn fiery red or a beech tree turn golden? It all comes down to chemistry. During the summer the leaves are full of chlorophyll, which harnesses energy from sunlight to combine water and carbon dioxide to create the sugars the leaves need to grow. The triggers for the seasonal change of hue include the drop in night-time temperatures and the fall in the number of daylight hours. As chlorophyll production ceases, the green pigment fades and the carotenoids (yellow/orange) and anthocyanins (red/purple) take over.

Some of our most colourful autumn foliage can be found in the beech forests of southern England, which turn orange and then gold in autumn. Then there are the yellows and russets of ash and oak, the reds of rowan and the exotic rainbow of pinks and purples on many non-native species from maples to ironwoods.

For exotic species, visit our parks and arboretums. For native favourites, including beech, alder, oak, ash, field maple and cherry, visit our woodlands. Top of the arboretum list is Westonbirt, The National Arboretum in Tetbury, Gloucestershire, home to around 2,500 different tree species.

Winkworth Arboretum in Surrey offers dazzling displays at the yellow to red end of the spectrum. In the first half of the 20th century, the dermatologist turned arboreal visionary Dr Wilfrid Fox chose the purples and reds of liquidambar (sweet gum), the golden yellows of hickory and tulip, and the copper and crimson of Japanese maple for Winkworth.

Stourhead in Wiltshire, one of the world's finest landscape gardens, begins its show at the end of August when the North American maples begin to turn scarlet red. They are soon followed by the Japanese acers, hornbeam and chestnuts, while oak and beech end the season in late October.

Both the Forest of Dean in Gloucestershire and the New Forest in Hampshire are renowned for their autumn glory. In Grizedale, between Coniston and Windermere in the Lake District, larch, oak, elder and beech create an unforgettable backdrop to the forest's famous woodland sculptures. These range from giant birds and mythical figures to a *trompe l'oeil* elephant on a rock.

Autumn Fungi

The Wood Wide Web

For most people the word 'fungi' refers to the profusion of oddly shaped mushrooms that appear, apparently out of nowhere, in woods and meadows during autumn. In fact, the parts we can see are just the fruiting bodies of a secret underground world of minuscule tendrils that form vast communication systems – dubbed the 'Wood Wide Web' by scientists – which provide our trees with the nutrients they need to survive.

This structure of fine root-like mycelium, sometimes up to 1,500 years-old, is one of nature's most complex networks of organisms; a network that recycles up to 90 per cent of dead and decaying matter in the natural world, including vast numbers of autumn leaves. Underneath the forest floor lie several tons of fungal material per acre which, as the soil becomes damper in autumn, produces the many thousands of fungi that spread their spores on the wind.

It is estimated that the UK is home to around 15,000 species of fungi. These are most abundant in unfarmed grasslands and in our woods, protruding from ancient tree trunks. Closely associated with our ancient folklore due to their array of fantastical shapes, sizes, colours, textures and patterns – not to mention their sometimes poisonous and hallucinogenic side effects – fungi have acquired enigmatic names more suggestive of a book of fairy tales than a book of botany.

These names include the scarlet elf cup, jelly ear, shaggy inkcap, death cap, orange peel fungus, parrot waxcap and the collared earthstar. The top prizes for appearance, smell and toxicity go to the phallic-shaped stinkhorn, the black protuberances of dead man's fingers and the red-and-white spotted cap of the fly agaric, whose hallucinogenic effects are said to have sent the invading Vikings into a frenzy.

On the flip side, the tastiest edible wild mushrooms that can be foraged in autumn include oyster mushrooms, with cream-coloured oyster-shaped caps

that frequently grow in tiers on the trunks of deciduous trees; giant puffballs that have a nutty, earthy taste; chanterelles, often found near beech or birch trees, with a peach-like scent and rich flavour; and the chunky cep or penny bun which has a strong mushroomy flavour.

Always remember when foraging for fungi that some species are very poisonous, while others are legally protected, meaning you could receive six months' imprisonment and a fine for picking them. During autumn, there are many organised fungi foraging walks led by experts, and this is one of the best ways to learn.

Two National Trust properties that are renowned for rare fungi – best left untouched – are the Tyntesfield Estate near Bristol and Sheringham Park in Norfolk. The former is home to more than 1,000 species, including its colourful waxcaps, which can be seen in abundance in October on the lawns around the ornate Gothic Revival house.

Wild Orchids

A Deceptive Beauty

The complexity, diversity and sheer exuberant beauty of the orchid family have bewitched botanists and plant lovers for centuries. A few years after the publication of *On the Origin of Species* in 1859, Charles Darwin published what he called his 'orchid book'. The objective was to prove how his theory of natural adaptation applied to flora as well as fauna. He did this by demonstrating how some species of orchid are pollinated by insects that are tricked into thinking they are mating with their own species.

An excellent example is the bee orchid, a relatively common species, which poses as a female bee trying to attract a mate. And you certainly don't have to be a bee to notice the resemblance. The flowers are quite large for an orchid,

with several growing on one stem. They have pink outer 'sepals' (petals), while the inner formation is a furry structure that resembles the yellow and brown body of a female bee. Just for good measure, two more dangling pollen sacs, or pollinia, look like the bee's antennae.

Seek one out, kneel down – they are usually about 6in (15cm) high – and while taking care not to cause any damage, examine the flower close-up. Just below the 'antennae', above the smiling mouth in the centre of the flower, you will see two brown dots – look straight into these eyes and you will be hypnotised in an instant. In one of nature's great ironies, the species of bee required to pollinate this extraordinary plant doesn't exist in Britain. So, just to be on the safe side, the bee orchid evolved to self-pollinate as well. Problem solved.

Another pollination strategy, Darwin noted, is that some orchids lure insects with the promise of sweet-smelling nectar, whereas others suggest exactly the same reward, but fail to come up with the goods. An open-and-shut case of unashamed 'food deception' whose evolution Darwin was unable to explain, and which still causes controversy among scientists to this day.

While it is estimated there are a staggering 169,000 cultivated hybrid species of orchid found in Britain, only 52 species exist in the wild, of which only nine are widespread. The common spotted orchid, for example, can be found everywhere from roadside verges and hedgerows to sand dunes and marshes, sometimes covering wide areas. Its pink flowers are densely packed in short, cone-shaped clusters. Other common species include the green-winged orchid, the twayblade orchid, the marsh orchid, the pyramidal orchid and the fragrant orchid.

Orchids begin flowering in April (early purple) and continue until August (pyramidal) and, in rare cases, October (autumn lady's tresses) with the best displays in May, June and July. Bee orchids are widespread throughout southern England, flowering in June and July and favouring dry, chalk or limestone grasslands. Top sites include Minchinhampton and Rodborough Commons near Stroud in Gloucestershire, and coastal areas such as Oxwich Bay on the Gower Peninsular.

Autumn lady's tresses, a stunning white spiral orchid, can be found in areas of grassland such as the National Trust's Golden Cap Estate on the Jurassic Coast in Dorset. They are also found across Hampshire, Sussex and Kent, reaching as far north as Yorkshire and the Cumbrian coast. One rare example is the early spider orchid, which can be found to the west of Dancing Ledge, a famous beauty spot at the southern end of the Isle of Purbeck, also in Dorset.

Wild Daffodils

The Trials of Narcissus

According to Greek mythology, after rejecting the love of the nymph Echo, the handsome youth Narcissus was lured to a pool by Nemesis, the goddess of revenge. A prophecy in childhood had meant Narcissus had never been allowed to see his own image, and he promptly fell in love with his reflection. In some versions of the myth, he leans over too far in an effort to get a better view of himself, topples in, and is drowned; in others, he pines away or kills himself. All renditions end with his transformation into the stunningly beautiful flower that came to be known as the daffodil.

For many of us, the idea of spending eternity as a flower, returning to life each spring in an explosion of colour, might seem quite an attractive

proposition. But for the man regarded as the original narcissist, our inability to distinguish him from the millions of gaudy imitators that have spread across the world to western and southern Europe as well as large parts of North America, Australia and New Zealand, must be hard to take.

While, for many, a daffodil is just a daffodil, on closer inspection you will see huge variations in their colour and shape. In fact, almost all of the bright yellow flowers that nod so beguilingly at us along the roadsides are one of the garden cultivars that have spilled over from their original homes and are in danger of condemning the truly wild daffodil to hybridised oblivion.

Once you know the difference between Narcissus himself (the wild daffodil, *Narcissus pseudonarcissus*) and his many imitators, he is easy to spot. His outer crown is made up of pale yellow petals (known as tepals) surrounding a darker yellow corona – the inner cup or trumpet. Daffodil hybrids and cultivars now include reds, oranges, pinks and whites, and have seduced our horticulturalists to such an extent that there are now an estimated 27,000 garden cultivars from a gene pool of more than 50 daffodil species. Wild daffodils are also shorter than their pretenders, with long, narrow,

grey-green leaves. They also have a tendency to grow in evenly distributed clumps, rather than as individual plants.

Happily, there are sites where the wild daffodil still thrives and can be seen at its best between March and April. These include: the north-eastern edge of Dartmoor, around Dunsford, along the River Teign in Devon; the Lake District (Brigsteer Woods, near Sizergh Castle); the North York Moors (Farndale, or 'Daffodil Dale', along the River Dove); the Black Mountains in Wales; and the area of countryside, woods and pastures known as the 'Golden Triangle' along the northern border of Gloucestershire (Dymock Woods) and the adjacent sections of southern Herefordshire and Worcestershire.

Perhaps most famous of all is the field next to Rydal Mount near Ambleside in Cumbria, home of the poet William Wordsworth, which he eventually gave to his daughter, Dora. When she died from tuberculosis at the age of 42, he planted it with wild daffodils in her memory. In March, the field, now cared for by the National Trust, is covered with thousands of yellow blooms – a fitting memorial to a beloved daughter from the poet who immortalised the 'golden daffodils' in his poem, 'I Wandered Lonely as a Cloud' (c. 1804).

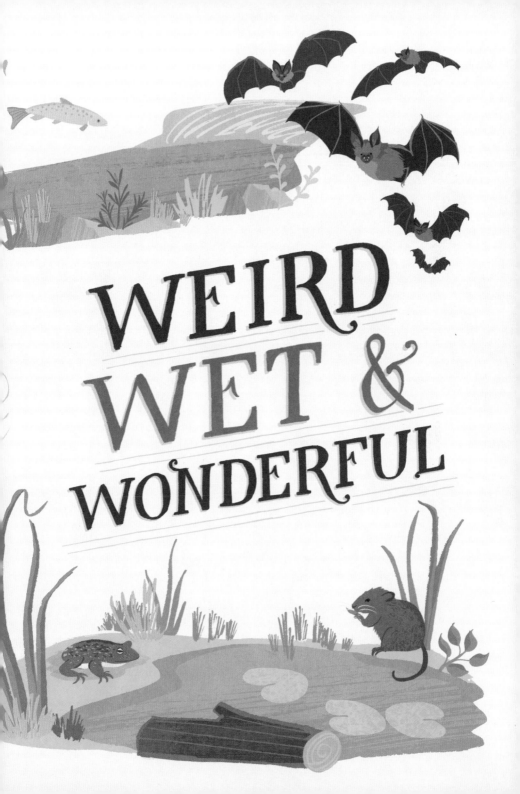

WEIRD
WET &
WONDERFUL

Rock Pooling

Meet the In-betweeners

It is the archetypal image of traditional family seaside holidays: shrimping nets packed in the car alongside the buckets and spades; the slippery paddle and clamber among the rock pools as the tide retreats; and the careful pushing aside of curtains of bladderwrack and sea lettuce in the hunt for strange creatures of the in-betweener world of the inter-tidal zone.

Suddenly, one is discovered, hiding deep in a crevice, but now revealed in all its goggle-eyed glory. The shout goes up: 'Look at this everyone!' The excitement is palpable and identification is at last confirmed: it is a shanny, a saucer-eyed sea frog with thick smiling lips and fan-like fins, also known as a blenny. Limpets, anemones and whelks are all very well, but this ranks alongside a bright orange starfish and even a sea-horse. Well … almost.

The pleasure of rock pools is that you never know quite what you might find in this liminal realm stranded between one world and the next. These creatures are exposed to an ever-changing habitat with varying water temperature and oxygen levels, surging tides and calm interludes. This universe of bizarre and seemingly exotic fish, invertebrates, crustaceans and marine plants includes yellow-spotted strawberry anemones and snakelocks anemones, hermit crabs, shore crabs and velvet crabs, rock gobies, pipe fish that look like swimming shoelaces, eels, sea scorpions, spiny starfish, sucker fish and butterfish.

The key to a successful rock pooling expedition is first to check the weather forecast and tide tables. Arrive a couple of hours before low tide when the sea is on its way out – between late spring and early autumn is best. Choose a calm day and time your visit to coincide with a low spring tide – the days near a full or new moon – for optimum conditions. To find the strangest and the most wonderful creatures, follow the tide out to its lowest point and explore the nearest exposed pools and crevices.

Useful items of kit include an identification guide, a hand lens, non-slip footwear and appropriate clothing for the weather, including sunscreen if needed; pack a first-aid kit too, in case of any bumps or scrapes. Try and leave those shrimping nets in the car, as they can knock seaweed off the rocks and creatures can get tangled up in them. Instead, use a bucket or a reusable box to scoop up your finds, and return everything to where it came from after you've identified your catch.

Rock pooling hotspots include Wembury Bay, near Plymouth, in Devon. The rocks in this area mostly comprise 400-million-year-old slate and sandstone that crack easily, providing the nooks and crannies for creatures to hide in and lay their eggs. Wembury Marine Centre runs regular rock pool rambles for children during the school holidays.

Further along the south coast is Kimmeridge Bay on the Isle of Purbeck, which also has the oldest marine nature reserve in the UK, with an excellent visitor centre. The rock pools at the base of the chalk cliffs of the Seven Sisters in Sussex are also a prime place for the dedicated rock pooler, while in the north of England, South Landing on Flamborough Head in Yorkshire, famous for its seabird colonies, is remarkable for its shoreside biodiversity.

Natterjack Toads

Lamborghini of the Amphibian World

Warm evenings in late spring are a perfect time to enjoy the vast, sandy estuary of the River Duddon in Cumbria where it flows into the North Sea. Across the bay, the mountains of Cumbria's Southern Fells stretch north towards Scafell Pike, providing a dramatic backdrop for the sand dunes of Sandscale Haws National Nature Reserve.

Over 600 plant species grow in this highly specialised habitat, including bee, northern marsh and coralroot orchids and wild pansies. A wealth of birdlife can be seen and heard overhead: waders, such as the ringed plover, dunlin and sanderling; raptors, including hen harriers and buzzards; and song birds such as skylarks and meadow pipits.

As dusk falls, another noise may be apparent among the dunes: a loud, rasping 'eeerk, eeerk, eeerk'. It is truly bizarre and disorientating, a sound reminiscent of the African savannas, or a tropical rainforest in South America – certainly not one associated with a stroll along the north-west coast of England.

An attempt to trace the origin of the sound is likely to lead to a pond among the dunes, where the noise will get louder ... and louder ... and louder. There, half-in, half-out of the water, sits a strange-looking creature. Every few seconds, its chin expands like a balloon, which looks as if it is about to burst. Instead, it lets out a call that can be heard by other toads up to 2 miles (3.2km) away.

The natterjack toad is one of the UK's rarest amphibians. It is smaller than the common toad, with a telltale yellow stripe running down its spine and dark warts on its back, often with yellow or red tips. It has much smaller legs than its cousin which, as well as making it an efficient excavator, also make it a very fast runner, earning it the epithet of 'the Lamborghini of the amphibian world' from wildlife expert Chris Packham. Its shimmering eyes are tinged with green, rather than the familiar orange of the common toad, and it can also darken or lighten its skin to camouflage itself against predators such as crows and seagulls.

The natterjack thrives in the warm shallow ponds of dune systems, coastal saltmarshes and lowland heaths, which often dry up completely in the heat of summer. Unsurprisingly perhaps, it is the male that is responsible for the loud calls heard between late March and June, in a bid to attract females during the mating season.

Sandscale Haws National Nature Reserve in Cumbria is thought to be home to around a quarter of the country's entire natterjack toad population, which is estimated at around just 4,000 individuals. These are found at coastal sites around the UK, most in the north of England (Formby in Merseyside, Cumbria, Lincolnshire) and the west coast of Scotland (Solway). Other natterjack sites include the Talacre dunes in north-east Wales and Holme Dunes National Nature Reserve in Norfolk, where The Wash meets the North Sea.

Butterflies

Beacons of Summer

The past is a foreign country. They have more butterflies there. And if you don't believe me, just browse the pages of a Victorian child's picture book. Every garden, it seems, was awash with them. Even today, summer only really comes alive when that kaleidoscope of colour in the form of tortoiseshells, red admirals and painted ladies descends on a bramble patch in full bloom.

Like colours themselves, everyone has a favourite. There is the exotic swallowtail with its yellow wings, black veins and blue tail flecks. It is our largest native butterfly, but also one of the rarest, only to be found flying above the reed beds of the Norfolk Broads. The male Adonis blue has brilliant sky-blue wings, while the peacock is resplendent with its spectacular pattern

of eyespots that startle or confuse predators. There is also the rarely seen purple emperor, restricted to the woodlands of southern England, and usually only glimpsed flying high in the treetops.

The charity Butterfly Conservation works hard to increase awareness of how much butterflies matter. There are many reasons to value our fluttering friends: they are key indicators of a healthy ecosystem, and long-term studies of them have proved extremely important for scientific research into climate change; they also have a rare and delicate beauty and act as powerful symbols of nature conservation for young people.

Every year in July and August, Butterfly Conservation conducts a Big Butterfly Count – a citizen science project used to assess the health of our environment by counting the number and type of butterflies around the whole of the UK. The data is then analysed for its five-year 'state of the nation' assessment of the UK's butterflies. Extraordinary features are still being discovered about butterflies. For example, they have a type of heart in their ultra-thin wings that pumps around their equivalent of blood (haemolymph) to keep them cool in summer and warm in winter.

In Britain, there are 57 resident species alongside two common migrants – the painted lady and the clouded yellow. Sadly, more than 40 of these species have declined dramatically in terms of numbers, distribution or both since 1980. On the plus side, around 25 have increased on both counts (Duke of Burgundy, pearl-bordered fritillary and dingy skipper, for example) and memorably, in 2009, an estimated 11 million painted ladies arrived in Britain from southern Europe, turning two Cornish fields into a cradle for perhaps half a million caterpillars.

Butterfly Conservation has more than 30 nature reserves around Britain, from Broadcroft Quarry, its most southerly, located in a disused limestone quarry on the Isle of Portland in Dorset, to Allt Mhuic on Loch Arkaig, north of Fort William in Scotland. Other excellent locations for finding butterflies in areas cared for by the National Trust include the chalk grasslands and woodlands of the Chiltern Hills (Oxfordshire, Buckinghamshire, Hertfordshire, Bedfordshire); Ashclyst Forest and Heddon Valley (Devon); Bookham Commons (Surrey); Compton Down (Isle of Wight); Noar Hill, Selborne (Hampshire); and Welshmoor, North Gower (Wales).

Glow Worms

The Lady with the Lamp

Raised in the far west of Cornwall in the 1960s, at a time when young children were often allowed to roam free after dark, some of my earliest experiences included night-time encounters with everything from badgers and foxes to hedgehogs and bats. Indeed, it is the sights and sounds of nature that conjure up my fondest memories of childhood.

Among the most vivid were the magical nights of midsummer, when the country lanes around our cottage were lit up by hundreds of pinpricks of light, as if the stars had fallen out of the sky and scattered themselves among the hedgerows in our remote river valley. To say I was mesmerised would be an understatement. Scanning the darkness with the smell of newly mown hay in my nostrils and the rhythmic chirrup of crickets in my ears was, for me, a real-life miracle.

When I was told that these miniature beacons were produced by worms, I felt not the slightest desire to find out what was really behind this amazing phenomenon – quite the reverse. As far as I was concerned, worms were confined to those wriggling pink things that slithered around in the jam jar in which my best friend used to keep his fishing bait. Fast forward many decades, and while my understanding of biology may have improved, the memory of that piece of natural magic has never diminished.

I now know that glow worms are not worms at all – they are beetles. *Lampyris noctiluca* is the species most often seen in the UK; the family name, Lampyridae, means 'shining ones' in Greek. The light is usually produced by the wingless female who, to help her attract a mate, has evolved the ability to produce two compounds, luciferin and luciferase, in the final two segments of her abdomen. These react to produce bioluminescence in the form of her trademark yellow-green glow, but with virtually no heat: 98 per cent of the energy produced is light.

The best time to observe this 'Lady with the Lamp' in all her glory is on dark moonless nights between late May and early September, with mid-June to mid-July usually being the most fruitful. You will see her soon after night falls, until about an hour after midnight. If children are with you, don't be surprised if you too catch a fleeting glimpse of shimmering fairy wings.

The glow worm is found in England (particularly the south), lowland Scotland and Wales. Her favourite haunts are gardens, woodland glades, hedges, churchyards, river banks, clifftops and moorland – usually near to the ground in short grass, but sometimes hidden among tussocks and plant stems. National Trust glow worm sites include Brownsea Island in Dorset (the evening displays are an exclusive treat for people staying in the Trust's holiday cottages on the island) and Stockbridge Down in Hampshire. The National Park Authorities and the County Trust for Nature Conservation also organise glow worm walks and publish information about local sightings.

Water Voles

Tails of the Riverbank

Immortalised as Ratty in the children's classic *The Wind in the Willows* (1908), the water vole on which Kenneth Grahame based his character has been loved by generations of children for its extroverted, friendly personality and knowledge of river life. In reality, this energetic ball of brown fur with its little round face, tiny ears, beaver-like incisors and twitching nose and whiskers, is just as charismatic and invaluable as a member of our riverine ecosystems.

Water voles live in networks of tunnels along the banks of rivers, streams, lakes and waterways, in reedbeds and areas of wet moorland with wide margins of lush vegetation where there aren't too many trees. They are nervous animals and so often difficult to spot, but their presence is easy to detect from the piles of nibbled stalks they leave behind, the ends cut off at a telltale 45 degrees. These make up part of their vegetarian diet in which they consume 80 per cent of their body weight on a daily basis. Nearby, you are likely to find the entrances to their burrows – about the size of a cricket ball – flanked by grazed 'lawns' of vegetation.

Sadly, the water vole is the UK's fastest-declining water mammal. A huge conservation effort is now underway to save them from further falls in population. A combination of habitat destruction, pollution and predation by imported American mink, which have escaped from fur farms, has led to a 95 per cent drop in water vole numbers since 1945.

To combat this reduction, water voles are now being bred in captivity and then released into locations where they were previously abundant. A notable example is Malham Tarn in the Yorkshire Dales, England's highest freshwater lake, where the National Trust introduced 100 water voles in both 2016 and

2017. Today the population has spread over a considerable area. The presence of otters, which keep the mink at bay, has also aided successful reintroduction.

At Malham Tarn, National Trust rangers have reported that the water voles rapidly changed the look of the tarn-side streams that used to be straight-sided, almost like canals. By burrowing into the banks, the voles have created more natural-looking streams, with shady pools that encourage invertebrates and small fish, demonstrating once again that healthy ecosystems can only be created by healthy wildlife. Their browsing on river banks can completely change the composition and structure of these environments.

Water voles spend the winter underground (inactive but not hibernating), and usually emerge between February and September, with August being a good month to see them in family groups. Original or reintroduced water vole strongholds include RSPB Rainham Marshes in the Thames Estuary; the Holnicote Estate in Exmoor National Park; Kielder Forest in Northumberland; and Thorley Wash on the River Stort, on the Hertfordshire and Essex border.

The Salmon Run

Nature's Homing Instinct

Nature can be a hard taskmaster – no more so than in the case of the Atlantic salmon (*Salmo salar*). When the time comes their primal instinct is to swim hundreds of miles from the middle of the ocean to breed in the headwaters of the river where they were born. But nature's imperatives, for all their harshness, have provided a compelling autumn spectacle among the waterfalls of some of our most beautiful rivers.

The life of an Atlantic salmon begins in the freshwater rivers where they hatch and remain for around three years. Leaving in the spring, the young 'smolt' swim downriver, slowly acclimatising to the salinity of the Atlantic, where they spend another four years in the waters off Norway and Greenland.

Here there are fewer predators and a far better food supply, which enables the salmon to grow into impressive athletes weighing up to 40lb (18kg) – necessary for making the Herculean journey back upriver.

The miraculous navigation systems salmon have evolved to make this journey possible are still not fully understood. Most experts believe that they tune into the Earth's magnetic field using microscopic crystals of magnetite in their flesh. This enables them to find the exact spawning ground, known as a redd, where they originally hatched.

During the long journey upriver, the salmon do not eat, becoming thinner and thinner in the process. Their head shape changes as their elongated jaws form a hook shape called a 'kype'. The males can be identified by their rosier flanks, while the females are darker, with the hint of a rainbow on their sides.

At times, when watching from above a waterfall, it looks as though the salmon are defying gravity, as flashes of silver shoot out of the foam like arrows, reaching heights as much as four times their own body length, before they wiggle and bend in mid-air as they return to the water. Few seem to make the required leap first time, but failure is not an option for a creature facing nature's demand to procreate.

When the salmon finally reach their goal, the females carve a shallow indentation in the gravel and lay a huge clutch of eggs, which the males then fertilise with their milt (sperm) – a process that is repeated several times. But their efforts usually come at the cost of their own lives. Only one in ten make it back to sea to repeat the process.

The timing of the salmon run each year is always slightly different, depending on how much rain has fallen. It is the amount of water in the rivers that provides the perfect conditions – not too much, not too little – that are necessary to bridge any obstacles the fish may encounter.

October and November are usually peak months. Top locations to take in this spectacle include Gilfach Nature Reserve in Powys on the River Marteg in Mid Wales; Stainforth Force on the River Ribble in the Yorkshire Dales; and Force Falls in Grizedale Forest in Cumbria. In Scotland, the River Almond (Buchanty Spout), the Linn of Tummel (the confluence of the rivers Garry and Tummel) in Perthshire, Crathes Castle in Aberdeenshire, Mar Lodge on the River Dee and Ettrick Weir on the River Tweed, are all usually excellent viewing locations.

Bats

Caped Crusaders

Bats are often unfairly maligned, perhaps due to their affinity with the night and darkness. We humans have long associated them with vampires, witchcraft and all things Hallowe'en. So it may be surprising that only three out of the world's estimated 1,200 bat species feed on blood alone. And none of them live in Britain.

In fact, bats bring us nothing but blessings. Without them, the natural world would be immeasurably poorer. We owe the beauty of our flowers and the nourishment of our fruits as much to bats as we do to bees. As well as being world-class pollinators and seed dispersers, they do us the favour of controlling garden pests, with Britain's most common bat, the tiny pipistrelle, downing as many as 3,000 insects in a single night. In Britain, all bat species and their roosts are legally protected, which means it is a criminal offence to harm a bat, or disturb or damage their roosts or breeding sites.

Famously, bats use echolocation – high-pitch sonar beyond the range of human hearing – to navigate the world around them when they leave their roosting sites to hunt at night. This phenomenal piece of natural technology allows them to 'see' in pitch darkness. They also have the ability to manoeuvre with such precision that they are able to home in on individual flying insects and catch them in their claws, before devouring each tasty morsel with their razor-sharp teeth. Bats are able to see perfectly well in daylight – it's just that they prefer to sleep most of the time instead.

Bats live in our towns and cities as well as our countryside, as near as possible to their preferred hunting grounds – the parks and green spaces, gardens, woods and bodies of water where insect populations are greatest.

Of the 17 bat species that breed in Britain, some are both very secretive and very rare. Most of us will only ever know what they look like close-up from photographs. But even just a fleeting glimpse and a large dose of imagination can be thrilling enough. Of the more common species, the brown long-eared bat with its 1-in (2.5-cm) long ears is among the most endearing, while the noctule bat is the UK's largest specimen, roosting mostly in trees, and flying high and fast in search of its favourite snack, flying beetles.

Many of us have experienced bats flitting past us in that haunting 'now you see them, now you don't' way of theirs, but heading out at dusk armed with a bat detector, an instrument that picks up the ultrasonic sounds of the bat and converts them into sounds you can hear and identify, is an altogether more vivid experience. It still doesn't mean you will necessarily see what you know is there. But your heart will definitely beat faster. Many wildlife organisations and local bat groups run bat walks where you can try out a detector.

Bats usually hibernate during the winter months, so are mostly seen between April and October, with their peak between June and August. They are easiest to see at sunset and sunrise during warm, dry weather.

Bat hotspots include the London Wetland Centre in south-west London and the Stackpole Estate on the coast of Pembrokeshire, home to the largest colony of horseshoe bats in Wales. The Threave Estate, cared for by the National Trust for Scotland, supports eight different bat species and offers guided walks.

Bottlenose Dolphins

Gymnasts of the Ocean

Few wildlife encounters inspire such raucous excitement as the breaching display of a pod of dolphins. Along with the sheer visual delight of watching these gymnasts of the ocean leaping out of the water or riding the bow waves of ships and boats, is the instinctive feeling that these air-breathing mammals are doing it primarily for just one simple reason: fun! And fun, even according to the scientists who study them, is the most likely explanation.

The bottlenose is the most common of the world's dolphin species and the most frequently seen in British waters. Bottlenose dolphins are recognisable from their dark grey backs, pale grey flanks and light underbelly. They get their name from their short, stubby beaks, like the neck of a bottle. These aren't actually their 'noses', as they breathe through the blowhole on the top of their heads and have no sense of smell at all. Individuals can be identified by the shape and markings of their dorsal fin, which is as unique as a human fingerprint.

Dolphins are extremely intelligent and sociable creatures, with brains that are bigger than our own. They communicate using a combination of squeaks, whistles and clicks and, like bats, use echolocation to detect prey. When they sleep, only one side of their brain shuts down, while the other stays aware of their surroundings, with one eye always open. The females are exclusively responsible for childcare, staying with their calves for up to six years. Scientists have recorded their young responding to whistles, like a name, which are unique to each individual.

Pods of bottlenose dolphins can be seen around the UK throughout the year – with the best sightings in summer – at both the Moray Firth and Aberdeen Harbour on the east coast of Scotland. Another well-known site is

Cardigan Bay on the west coast of Wales, where a permanent population lives around the harbour town of New Quay. They can also be spotted all along the coastline between the Llŷn Peninsula in the north and Strumble Head in north Pembrokeshire. The coast of Cornwall and the Scilly Isles off Land's End are other hotspots.

Due to the coldness of the water, the largest, chunkiest and darkest bottlenose dolphins in the world are found around the coasts of Scotland. Individuals measuring up to 13ft (4m) have been recorded. Boat trips on the Moray Firth often provide superb views of the dolphins breaching. It is equally exciting to see them chasing Atlantic salmon towards the shore on the incoming tide from the spit behind Chanonry Point Lighthouse.

Another place to spot Moray's bottlenose dolphins is at the Scottish Dolphin Centre, based in an 18th-century salmon fishing station at the mouth of the River Spey. The area is a nature reserve, home to dolphins as well as other mammals, including red squirrels, pine martens and seals, plus a variety of seabirds such as skuas, cormorants and turnstones.

Basking Sharks

Open-mouthed Leviathans

Few creatures are more likely to trigger a heart-stopping moment than a
basking shark. First, there is its sheer size. Measuring around 33ft (11m)
in length and weighing 5 tons, the basking shark is the second largest fish
in the world after the whale shark.

But it doesn't stop there: the basking shark's most astonishing feature is
its vast, cavernous mouth. With a diameter of more than 3ft (almost 1m), it
is large enough to hold a scuba diver in full kit. Frequently mistaken for sea
monsters in past centuries, basking sharks are in fact among the most docile
of creatures, posing no danger to snorkellers or divers.

Surprisingly perhaps, the mouth of the basking shark did not evolve to
consume the largest meal it can find, but instead the smallest. It feeds on

some of the most minuscule creatures in the oceans: zooplankton. Most of these organisms are invisible to the naked eye, but by swimming passively with its mouth open, the basking shark filters the water with comb-like structures known as gill-rakers, located inside the huge gills that encircle its head. When feeding, a volume of water equivalent to around three-quarters of an Olympic-sized swimming pool passes through its mouth every hour.

Often seen swimming slowly near the surface of the water, it was once thought that this gentle creature was basking in the sun – hence its common name. Later this was identified as feeding behaviour, which is exactly what it still does during the summer months. This primarily takes place on the west coast of Britain, from Cornwall heading north to the east coast of Ireland (Rathlin Island), the Hebrides (Isle of Coll near Mull) and beyond.

The shark's huge size means it can be seen from coastal cliffs, identified by its triangular-shaped fins – one in the middle of its back (dorsal) and the other on its tail (pectoral). They are most often seen on flat, calm days in good weather, when the shoals of plankton are closest to the surface. Sightings usually start in May and tail off in September, with peak activity from the end of July to mid-August.

Cornwall is arguably the best place in Britain to snorkel or dive with basking sharks due to its clear waters. However, the greatest numbers can be seen off the south-west of the Isle of Man, where they are regularly spotted within a mile of the land along a 35-mile (56-km) stretch of coastline.

Sadly for such a large and gentle creature, the basking shark has been the victim of harmful legal and illegal fishing practices. Although now protected in British and European waters, basking sharks are still hunted in other parts of the world for their skin (leather), fins (soup) and liver (oils for cosmetics).

The conservation status of the basking shark was changed from Vulnerable to Endangered on the IUCN Red List of Threatened Species in 2018. Along with legal protection in the UK and Europe, and recognition by global organisations such as the United Nations Convention on the Law of the Sea (UNCLOS) and the Convention on International Trade in Endangered Species of Wild Fauna and Flora (CITES), the Shark Trust has established the Basking Shark Project that invites shark enthusiasts to record their sightings and share information so that conservation efforts can be improved.

Whales

Goliaths of the Deep

Like humans, they breathe air. Like humans, they feed their offspring with breast milk. Like humans, they nurture their young and teach them life skills. Like humans, they socialise and work together in groups. They can even sing. And, according to a ground-breaking study by cetacean biologists Hal Whitehead and Luke Rendell, some even develop cultural habits of their own, passing on and evolving their mating songs and feeding habits over time.

There are two main groups of whales: baleen whales and the smaller, faster toothed whales. The former filter their food (plankton, krill and crustaceans) through the dense curtains of bristly fibres in their mouths, while the latter feed on larger marine prey (fish, squid and even seals) using their teeth.

Although mostly associated with faraway oceans, many whale species live in the seas around Britain. These include minke, humpback, sperm, fin and the killer whale or orca. The most common of these is the minke whale, one of the smallest species of baleen whale, which is identified by its shiny dark grey skin and white underbelly, pointed snout and large white patch on its flippers. Like all baleen whales, it has two blowholes.

Minke whales can be seen in the North Sea between Seahouses (Northumberland) and Whitby (North Yorkshire) from late June to October, when they come to feed off the shoals of herring that are plentiful at this time. They can often be seen from land, but the best chance to see them is on a whale-watching cruise from the port of Whitby, with the added chance of spotting fin, sei and humpback whales, as well as dolphins.

Humpback whales grow to 40–50ft (12–15m) long and weigh more than 40 tons. Their flippers can measure up to one-third of their entire body length which, along with their giant fanned tails, help them migrate as far as 16,000 miles (almost 26,000km) a year, from their feeding grounds in the polar latitudes to their breeding grounds in the tropics. Humpbacks are renowned for their acrobatic displays that include energetic head breaches and fin slapping, as well as raising their tail flukes high out of the water – a signal that they are about to make a deep dive.

Sightings of humpback whales off British shores have been increasing in recent years, and they can most often be seen off the Outer Hebrides (St Kilda), the Shetland Islands (Sumburgh Head) and the Isles of Scilly while heading south in late summer from their feeding grounds off Iceland. On the Scottish mainland, Sanna Point on the Ardnamurchan Peninsula is a well-known site for spotting cetaceans.

Orcas, also known as killer whales, are unmistakeable with their black backs, white chests and white flashes down their sides and around their eyes, but sightings are rare. A group of four pairs, known as the West Coast Community, arrives off the Hebrides and the west coast of Scotland in early summer but has also been seen in the Moray Firth and off the coast of Wales.

The Sea Watch Foundation monitors whale populations around the UK and the condition of their habitats. Volunteers are encouraged to report their sightings, which are used to raise awareness and promote environmental change to help conserve and protect these phenomenal creatures.

NATURE
HOTSPOTS
& WILDLANDS

Wicken Fen

Wildness to Wilderness

The fens of East Anglia are known for their unique habitat and rare wildlife. Less well-known is the surprising fact that a group of 'tigers' were active around Wicken Fen, near Cambridge, during the 17th century.

In the 1630s, wealthy landowners led by the Earl of Bedford realised a fortune could be made by draining the vast landscape of the Cambridgeshire Fens and turning it over to agricultural land. If it hadn't been for the ferocious resistance of local villagers, who became known as the Fen Tigers, trying to protect their livelihoods – eel catching, fishing, wildfowling, cutting reeds and sedge for thatching and building materials – Wicken Fen too would have been destroyed.

By the end of the 17th century, drainage of the fens was largely complete. Along with 20th-century drainage and intensive farming, less than 1 per cent of a vast ecosystem of more than 2,500 sq. miles (6,475 sq. km) is left in its original form.

Victorian naturalists, including Charles Darwin, recognised the value of what remained of the undrained Cambridgeshire fens. Wicken Fen was a favourite place to come to build their collections, especially of rare beetles and moths. In 1899, the National Trust bought 2 acres (0.8ha) for £10 from one of these collectors, stepping in to save Wicken Fen from the constant threat of being drained, and creating what is now its oldest nature reserve. A century later, the Trust initiated its Wicken Fen Vision, a 100-year plan to increase the area to 20 sq. miles (52 sq. km), transforming wildness to wilderness for the benefit of future generations.

During the last 20 years, the reserve has already more than doubled in size to 2,000 acres (785ha) recreating priority habitats of wetland and reedbed. The reserve includes over 30 miles (48km) of footpaths, cycleways and bridleways, so that visitors can walk, cycle or ride horses through the landscape to reconnect with nature.

Wicken Fen provides a window onto a lost landscape, giving a fascinating insight into our biodiverse past. It is home to more than 9,000 species of plants, birds and mammals, including over 150 threatened species, among them the bittern, marsh harrier, great crested newt and the tiny soprano pipistrelle bat. You may also catch a tantalising glimpse of the Fen's many species of butterflies (commas, gatekeepers, meadow browns, green-veined whites), dragonflies (emperors, migrant and brown hawkers, banded demoiselles, darters) and damselflies (red-eyed, willow emerald, azure, blue-tailed).

Since the start of rewilding more than 20 years ago, many bird species, such as cranes, short-eared owls and lapwings, have returned. Even so, restoring the Fen to its original state is impossible without introducing species that can do the job of the people who once lived there. Highland cattle and Konik ponies have been introduced to help create an open habitat, naturally. Their grazing and movement spreads seeds, aiding pollination across the site.

The restoration of natural processes, along with careful management of water, will allow the land to evolve an even greater mosaic of habitats for its abundant wildlife, safeguarding its status as one of the most biodiverse ecosystems in the country.

Brownsea Island

A Sanctuary for Wildlife

It is sometimes easy to forget that Britain is a nation of islands. There are the larger ones that most of us live on, of course, but around the coasts there are thousands of others – most tiny and uninhabited, some bleak and windswept, and others warm and welcoming with protected coves and sandy beaches. Many are wildlife havens, with their own protected habitats. One of these is Brownsea Island in Poole Harbour, Dorset, on the south coast of England.

Brownsea is famous for being the location in 1907 of an experimental camp for children led by Lord Baden-Powell, which later led to the founding of the Scout and Guide Movements. Today, it is also known as a hugely popular and biodiverse nature reserve cared for by the National Trust and managed jointly with the Dorset Wildlife Trust.

Just 1 mile (1.6km) long, half a mile (0.8km) wide and easy to navigate along wildlife trails and boardwalks, Brownsea is reached by a 20-minute ferry ride from Poole Quay. As an introduction to wildlife it is hard to beat, with its population of more than 200 red squirrels and colonies of migrating seabirds – both major attractions for visiting groups of schoolchildren and families.

Red squirrels are now endangered in Britain, due to the loss of much of their woodland habitat, and the introduction of the American grey between the late 19th and early 20th centuries. The grey squirrel carries the squirrel pox virus, to which they are immune but is deadly for the reds. The good news is that Brownsea Island is one of the safest strongholds in the south of England for these rare creatures. Red squirrels are easiest to see in spring, when food becomes more plentiful, and autumn, when they are hoarding for winter. They are most active in the early morning and late afternoon.

More than one-third of all bird species seen in Britain have been spotted on Brownsea, with over 20,000 birds visiting Poole Harbour each year to feed and roost. In summer, these include large numbers of common and sandwich terns and rare species of gulls, while in winter the island is home to over-wintering populations of spoonbill and avocet, alongside flocks of waders, including black-tailed godwit, shelduck and oystercatcher.

There are eight priority habitats on Brownsea, which sustain a huge wealth of wildlife – from larger mammals, such as the herd of sika deer, to smaller residents such as the tiny pink crab spider. Sika deer were first introduced from Japan in the late 1800s when the island was privately owned. They are excellent swimmers, and stags have even been spotted swimming across the harbour from the mainland to mate with the females on the island.

Although the deer help to keep some areas maintained naturally, they have a detrimental impact on the grassland and woods of the island. Sadly, much of the habitat of the Dartford warbler established at the RSPB reserve on the Arne peninsula has been destroyed by the activities of wandering deer.

On the inland trails, there are more than 65 different types of tree, including native hardwood trees such as oak, beech, rowan and hazel, as well as the coniferous trees such as Scots and Maritime pine that are so important for the red squirrels.

Brownsea is open between mid-March and October. Pitches at the campsite on the south side of the island, overlooking the Purbeck Hills, can be booked in advance for both groups and individuals.

Blakeney Point

England's Largest Seal Colony

No one in possession of a beating heart can resist the face of a fluffy white seal pup. Anthropomorphism – the projection of human emotions onto animals – has probably done more to raise awareness of the plight of vulnerable species around the world than any amount of factual data. So, if you're not averse to a reminder, but would also like to witness a conservation success story, head for Blakeney Point National Nature Reserve.

Recognised internationally for the importance of its seal colonies and breeding birds, Blakeney is a 4-mile (6.4-km) spit of shingle that stretches east to west along the north coast of Norfolk. The spit, which has been slowly extending westwards for more than 1,000 years, protects Blakeney Harbour

and its adjacent salt marshes from the sometimes fierce weather blasting in from the North Sea.

Blakeney's seals are a mixed colony of harbour and grey seals. The harbour seals have their young between June and August, while the greys breed in winter, between late October and mid-January. Grey pups are famous for their fluffy white coats, and feed on their mother's milk for up to three weeks as they triple in size and gradually shed their fur. In 2001 just 25 pups were born, but numbers have now dramatically increased to more than 3,000 a year, making Blakeney the largest seal colony in England. Rare black-coloured pups have also been spotted at Blakeney. Known as melanistic seals, they count for around one in 400 grey seals and are born with a striking velvety black coat.

A team of rangers at the reserve protects and monitors the colony. Disturbance is a major issue and can lead to abandonment or the accidental crushing of the pups by the adults, which can be fatal. For the safety of both seals and visitors, the western-most mile of beach and dunes is fenced off during the breeding season. Pups are regularly counted, and any found to be seriously ill or injured are taken to the RSPCA hospital at East Winch.

The National Trust purchased the land and created the reserve – the first coastal nature reserve in Britain – in 1912. The iconic blue wooden Lifeboat House was added in 1922 and is now a visitor centre and accommodation for the rangers. From here they carry out their crucial scientific work, starting at 4am in the nesting season to monitor and protect the birds in the adjacent marshes.

Birds regularly seen in spring include skylarks, lapwings and redshank, followed by spectacular displays of breeding terns in high summer along with marsh harrier, lapwing and avocet. During the winter months, Blakeney provides a refuge for pink-footed and brent geese, as well as large numbers of wigeon and golden plover.

The Point is about as wild as it is possible to get in southern Britain. There are no roads, and the 3-mile (4.8-km) walk (one way) from the car park along the shingle spit is not for the faint-hearted. The best way to see the seals is to take one of the ferry trips that run several times a day from Morston Quay. The Norfolk Coast Path runs around the perimeter of the marshes and mudflats of Blakeney Freshes, protected from the sea by the shingle spit, with uninterrupted views of the reserve's bird colonies and the possibility of seeing other rare species such as otters and water voles.

Rutland Water

The Naturalist's Glastonbury

For most of the year, it's the stars of the birding firmament that visitors flock to see at Rutland Water Nature Reserve, the UK's largest man-made lake near Oakham in the East Midlands. In winter, the big draw is the reserve's 25,000 waterfowl. These include thousands of tufted duck, wigeon and coot as well as many hundreds of teal, mallard and shoveler. Rare migrants – we're often talking single figures, here – include the male smew, that exotic glam-rock star of the frozen north with its shaggy crest and black eye patches.

In spring, great crested grebes can be seen performing their elegant, synchronised mating dance. In summer, the waders take centre stage, feeding on the exposed mud together with large flocks of godwits, as well as stints, sandpipers and even spoonbills. Rutland's most famous inhabitants are its

ospreys. After being reintroduced in 1996, they later nested here before hatching the first chicks to fledge in central England for more than 150 years.

The hottest ticket of them all, however, is reserved for the third weekend in August when nature lovers, birdwatchers and wildlife enthusiasts from all corners of the globe come to Birdfair. First held in 1989, Birdfair is one of the biggest events of its kind in the world, often referred to as 'the naturalist's Glastonbury'. As well as providing a showcase for the birding world in general, along with the latest hi-tech optics and outdoors equipment, it hosts talks by celebrity naturalists while raising hundreds of thousands of pounds for international conservation projects.

Managed by the Leicestershire and Rutland Wildlife Trust in partnership with Anglian Water, Rutland Water was created in the 1970s when a dam was built at Empingham creating a reservoir to provide water for the East Midlands. At its western end, 500 acres (200ha) was set aside for a nature reserve, now expanded to 1,000 acres (400ha). The Rutland Water Nature

Reserve combines both the Egleton Nature Reserve in the west, a network of lagoons and wetlands, and the Lyndon Nature Reserve on the south shore, from where the ospreys can best be seen.

One of the best ways to see the ospreys is to take an early morning or evening summer cruise on the *Rutland Belle* in the company of members of the Rutland Osprey Project team. Early morning is a particularly magical time to be out on the reservoir, when the boat visits the locations that offer the best chance of seeing the birds swooping out of the sky while hunting for fish.

Rutland Water also has more than 30 birdwatching hides, connected by nature trails on the edge of the lake with superb views. Some of the best are over the Lyndon Nature Reserve, looking north towards Hambleton and beyond to Burley-on-the-Hill House – a Palladian mansion on the north shore. A team of knowledgeable volunteers and reserve experts are also usually on hand to answer questions and help with species identification.

Insh Marshes National Nature Reserve

Wetland Wonderland

For many, the word 'fenland' conjures up images of low-lying wetlands stretching towards the sea: not a bad description, in fact, of most fens in the UK. They are also beautiful landscapes, rich in wildlife and rare plants. Making up only about 3 per cent of the nation's landmass, they nonetheless contain about 10 per cent of its biodiversity.

But now think again and imagine such a place inland, alongside a river, bordered by snow-covered mountains 3,000ft (over 900m) high. In the autumn, sedges turn gold in the late sunshine, while along the marshy land towards the river, migrating whooper swans and greylag geese return from their summer holidays in Iceland. Meanwhile, hen harriers, with their distinctive black-tipped wings, circle in the skies above, ready to roost.

These are the Insh Marshes on the River Spey, in the west of the Cairngorms National Park in the Highlands of Scotland. The uplands to the north are the rugged Monadhliath Mountains, a remote area of high-altitude moorland between the Cairngorms and Loch Ness, haunt of both golden eagles and the extremely rare Scottish wild cat.

The Invertromie Trail, a waymarked trail almost 1 mile (1.5km) long, takes in three hides that look out over the marshes. It passes through a rare mix of habitats: stands of birch and aspen; riverside meadows; and heather moorland, which is home to ospreys and buzzards, as well as the dainty creature that was the inspiration for Felix Salten's 1928 book *Bambi* – the roe deer. More than 500 species of plants can be found here, such as orchids, pillwort, the yellow water lily and string sedge, the last of which can only be found in two other places in the UK.

This 6-mile (9.7-km) stretch of wetland floods mainly between November and April, when heavy rains or snowmelt from the surrounding mountains inundate the River Spey. It is considered one of the most important and least disturbed fenland landscapes in Europe. But perhaps the true stars of this

unique habitat are the wading birds that arrive in spring, including curlew, lapwing, redshank and snipe.

The curlew is Europe's largest shore bird, instantly recognisable by its long legs, trademark down-curved bill, speckled brown plumage and a mating call that sounds like bubbling water. The lapwing (or peewit as it is sometimes called – a name derived from its song) can easily be recognised by its exotic crest curling up from the back of its head. Its mating display is another noted characteristic: this involves a flight during which it climbs suddenly and then tumbles out of the sky, its wings creating a distinctive humming sound.

Managed by RSPB Scotland, the Insh Marshes are part of the Cairngorms Connect rewilding initiative. Its long-term vision is to completely restore the naturally functioning floodplain and river system. The recent introduction of a small herd of semi-feral Konik ponies from Eastern Europe, each with a characteristic black stripe along its spine and lower back, has lent another charismatic presence to the fenland. Their love of grazing on reeds helps maintain the wetlands and improves the conditions for nesting birds and other species.

Cwm Ivy

Shifting Shores

During the winter of 2013–14, savage storms and high winds hit the Gower Peninsula – that enchanted outcrop of land jutting out into the Bristol Channel, halfway along the soft underbelly of the Welsh coast. Cwm Ivy is a small envelope of marshland on the north coast of the Gower, an area known for its dunes, marshes and mudflats and as an internationally important feeding ground for wading birds and wildfowl.

At the time of the storms, Cwm Ivy was sheep-grazed farmland dotted with Corsican pine and willow trees. But, in the years since, nature has taken a decisive hand. Today it is a biodiverse salt marsh inhabited by species that range from ospreys and curlews to otters and polecats. So, what exactly brought about this astonishing transformation?

The story of Cwm Ivy as we know it began in the 17th century, when a sea defence was built along the coastline so that the land could be claimed for farming. By 2013, however, the continually refortified sea wall was showing signs of weakness. The pressure of the water had created a small hole under the wall, and the following winter of storms, rain and high tides widened the hole further, allowing significant amounts of sea water to flow through. The final blow came the following summer when the wall failed completely.

The National Trust, which cares for the land, was confronted with a dilemma. Should it try to rebuild the wall and drain the land once more, or face the reality of rising sea levels and unpredictable weather? The Trust concluded that constant reconstruction of coastal defences was no longer beneficial in the long term. The only possible conclusion was to allow nature to map its own future and for Cwm Ivy to remain undefended.

At first, the results were unedifying. What had been lush, green swathes of pasture the previous year became a quagmire of mud, dead grass and the skeletal remains of trees. Happily, this transition phase was temporary, and very soon, salt marsh plants started to take over. The results since then have been spectacular. Today, there is a fully established salt marsh at the heart of Cwm Ivy. Coastal wetlands are highly efficient stores of carbon: when marshland plants die, they become buried in mud that absorbs the carbon produced as they decompose. Rising sea levels then bring in more layers of sediment that lock away this carbon-rich material.

Seen from the surrounding limestone grasslands, Cwm Ivy is a jigsaw of different ecosystems. As well as the newly created salt marsh and reedbeds, there is woodland, some remaining sections of freshwater marsh with newts and frogs, and sand dunes along the coastal strip. The result is a dynamic coastal super habitat – just as nature originally intended.

At the root of this biodiversity are the colourful salt marsh plants that provide an annual feast of nectar and pollen for bees and butterflies, as well as seeds for the many birds that are now found here. Alongside the ospreys, these include lapwings, hen harriers and kingfishers. The marshland is also a haven for wildfowl feasting on marine invertebrates, and huge flocks of songbirds including meadow pipit, chaffinch and linnet.

Alladale Wilderness Reserve

Wilderness Reimagined

On the face of it, 'shifting baseline syndrome' (SBS) sounds like the cunning strategy of an unscrupulous politician. In fact, it is far more serious. 'Our human tendency is to perceive current conditions against a small set of recent reference points (or baseline), so we often do not recognise long-term environmental change,' is how Lizzie Jones, who studied the phenomenon for her PhD at Royal Holloway, University of London, defines it. 'Without experience or knowledge of past environmental conditions, each new generation interprets more degraded environmental conditions as the new norm.'

Take, for example, the Great Caledonian Forest, the vast expanse of forested wilderness that once covered more than 3.5 million acres (1.4 million ha) of the

Scottish Highlands. 'It would have been a mosaic of lichen, lush pine, birch, alder, rowan, willow and oak,' says Paul Lister, the visionary philanthropist who, since 2003, has been rewilding the Alladale Wilderness Reserve, his 23,000-acre (9,300-ha) estate north-west of Inverness. 'There would have been a dense forest. In it would have been wolves, bears, wild boar and lynx.'

For most visitors, and even some local families who have lived in the Highlands for generations, this comes as something of a revelation. SBS, it seems, has been gaining traction for centuries. In truth, only a small fraction of the original ancient forest remains, the trees felled and the wild animals hunted to local extinction to make way for sheep, cattle and the grouse moors of the traditional Scottish estates. Deer populations have also been allowed to escalate for hunting purposes, leading to overgrazing, which in turn prevents tree saplings from maturing.

While the definitions of both 'beauty' and 'wilderness' are subjective, it would be hard to describe the Alladale of today as anything other than very beautiful and very wild. For Lister, however, despite the grandeur of the surrounding hills and glens, it is a landscape that bears no relationship to what nature intended. In response, he and his team have planted a million trees in the reserve's two glens, Glen Mhor and Glen Alladale. Four thousand small dams have also been built to restore the ancient peat bogs that were once such

an effective carbon sink. He is also working with the Royal Zoological Society of Scotland to bring back species that have disappeared locally, including red squirrels, and white-tailed and golden eagles. A breeding programme for Scottish wildcats, which need woodland to survive, will also soon be boosting numbers of the critically endangered 'highland tiger'.

The most contentious of Lister's possible future plans is the reintroduction of megafauna such as wolves. In response to 'Wolf Man' media headlines and local farmers fearing predation on their sheep, Lister points out that there would only be two packs of wolves, which would be enclosed within an electric fence around the estate. If this project goes ahead, it is likely to be a considerable draw: in the USA, where wolves were reintroduced to Yellowstone National Park in 1995, $40 million a year in tourism revenue has been added to the local economy.

Visitors to Alladale can stay in a choice of three catered lodges for groups of between two and 30 guests. These include the main lodge, a five-star Victorian manor house with the views, atmosphere and fine dining of a royal hunting lodge of yesteryear, minus the guns and stag head trophies adorning the walls. Hiking and mountain biking are popular, alongside activities such as clay pigeon shooting and trout fishing. The highlight of a stay, however, is to witness at first-hand one of Europe's most important rewilding projects in action.

Knepp Castle Estate

The Call of the Wild

What happens when humans take their hands off the tiller and let nature decide the correct course to steer? In 2001, Charlie Burrell and Isabella Tree, owners of 3,500 acres (over 1,400ha) of former farmland around the River Adur in West Sussex, decided to find out. The results have been spectacular.

During the Second World War, the Knepp Estate played an important role in the Dig for Victory campaign, when huge swathes of southern Britain were given over to food production. But when Charlie inherited the estate in the 1980s, the post-war intensive farming model had only resulted in spiralling debt and an increasing monoculture devoid of wildlife and biodiversity.

Today, the Knepp Estate has become a byword for the magic that can happen when nature calls the shots. First, shrubs and thorns took the place of the

annual crops, followed by a resurgence of insect life and returning songbirds. Today, in summer, buzzards and peregrine falcons circle in thermals as the giant wings of white storks whir overhead, their beaks making a characteristic clacking sound as they come in to land in the surrounding trees.

In *Wilding*, her best-selling book about Knepp, Isabella Tree explains how the animals that have been introduced are proxies for the free-roaming animals that lived here thousands of years ago. The now extinct auroch, for example, was a giant species of longhorned cattle, which has now been replaced by the Old English variety; Exmoor ponies have replaced the ancient tarpan; and Tamworth pigs, wild boar.

The behaviour patterns of these modern-day inhabitants of Knepp are similar to their forbears. They are grazers and browsers, which open up niches for other life, resulting in an explosion of biodiversity. 'Let these free-roaming animals disturb, trample, rootle, snap branches,' Isabella says.

Chief among the rare or endangered species that now flourish at Knepp are the turtle doves known from the carol 'The Twelve Days of Christmas',

nightingales, cuckoos, exotic purple emperor butterflies and 13 out of the 18 species of UK bats. In spring, when a bird survey is conducted for 10 days in succession starting at 4.30am, the dawn chorus is deafening.

In the spring of 2020, after a licence was granted by Natural England, a new chapter in Knepp's evolution began when two pairs of beavers were released into the River Adur for the first time in 400 years. Beavers are incredibly effective at creating water systems that are able to purify and store water, and protect against devastating floods. Classified as a 'keystone species', beavers have a hugely beneficial effect on the surrounding ecosystem and the biodiversity they help to create and maintain.

Today, the Knepp Estate runs a profitable business producing organic, pasture-fed meat from its free-roaming herds of animals, combined with eco-tourism based around its safari campsite. In a world where a degraded natural environment has increasingly become the norm, rewilding offers real hope for the future of both the planet and the human spirit. Thankfully, the call of the wild has been answered at Knepp.

Glenfeshie Estate

A Landscape Reborn

For years the debate raged: would a reduction of deer numbers through culling lead to the regeneration of a forested Cairngorms landscape that had changed beyond all recognition since it came into being at the end of the last Ice Age around 12,000 years go? Even just 200 years ago, large parts of the Highlands were covered in pine, alder, birch and juniper, with a whole ecosystem of plants and wildlife that thrived under their cover. But the Victorian obsession with driven grouse shooting that followed denuded the landscape of much of its previous wildness and biodiversity.

Everything that was necessary for those ancient forests to rebuild themselves in the form of saplings and flowering shrubs had been grazed

into submission by the deer, whose existence in unsustainable numbers was encouraged by the traditional game-stalking economy. Then, in 2006, Anders Povlsen, the Danish fashion tycoon and conservationist, bought the Glenfeshie Estate in the heart of the Cairngorms National Park.

Glenfeshie is famous for being the location that inspired the Victorian landscape artist Sir Edwin Landseer when he painted *The Monarch of the Glen*, and where Queen Victoria herself stayed in the 1860s. Undeterred by its history as a deer-stalking epicentre, Povlsen was determined to return the estate to its former glory, while still retaining its sporting heritage. Since then, the Glenfeshie Estate, which covers 65 sq. miles (168 sq. km), has seen a reduction of deer numbers and a dramatic regeneration of natural habitats, including its peat bogs – a much-needed carbon sink in the face of the climate crisis – and wildflowers, native pinewoods and young trees.

More than 5,000 species have now been recorded at Glenfeshie, many of which are classified as rare or scarce, including golden eagles, wildcats, pine martens, ospreys, black grouse, ptarmigan and otters. The remaining native forests of the Cairngorms, which include those on the Glenfeshie Estate, are

now home to half the UK's population of male capercaillie, the world's largest grouse and a bird under serious threat in Scotland.

Povlsen went on to set up Wildland, a 200-year project to restore not only Glenfeshie, but also his 12 other Highland estates. Povlsen and his teams have since planted four million trees and Wildland is also now a driving force behind Cairngorms Connect, another long-term project coordinating the regeneration plans of adjoining estates and reserves from the River Spey and the Insh Marshes to the summit of Ben Macdui. This is a landscape that covers more than 230 sq. miles (596 sq. km) and includes ancient woodlands, rivers, lochs, peat bogs and wetlands, as well as the Cairngorm mountains themselves.

There is a renovated bothy (Ruigh Aiteachain) that offers free shelter to hikers exploring the estate. For those in need of more comfort, there are a number of cottages that can be rented, as well as the historic lodge that comes with its own chef and private staff.

Wild Ennerdale

A Living Laboratory

'I think sometimes there can be a misconception about the term "rewilding",' says Rachel Oakley, Partnership Officer for Wild Ennerdale. 'People sometimes think we're trying to create a past landscape. We're not trying to do that at all. It's very much about looking to the future. Our vision is to let Ennerdale evolve as a wild valley for the benefit of people but relying more on natural processes to shape its landscape and ecology than was the case in the past.'

Ennerdale is one of the most isolated, least known and wildest valleys in the Lake District, rising abruptly out of a coastal plain in the north-west of Cumbria. It is a spectacular upland landscape of woodlands, fells and

mountains connected by the River Liza – one of the purest and most pristine rivers in England – and Ennerdale Water, a 2-mile (3.2-km) glacial lake.

The area is most often associated with Pillar Rock, a huge crag on the flanks of Pillar Mountain itself at the remote eastern end of the valley, regarded as the birthplace of rock climbing in the Lakes and first climbed in 1826. It is also known in archaeological circles for its prehistoric and medieval sites stretching back 5,000 years to the Bronze Age. Its wide range of habitats includes everything from sub-alpine to lakeshore, wetland, grassland and forest ecosystems.

While still remote and beautiful, by the turn of the last century Ennerdale had been blighted by the twin scourges of extensive conifer cultivation, planted for timber production after the Second World War, and by over-grazing of sheep. The swathes of conifers caused a huge drop in biodiversity by depriving the forest floor of natural light and stifling the growth of native trees, plants and vegetation with blankets of pine needles.

In 2002, realising that the valley could be managed better for the benefit of both people and nature, the principal landowners in the valley formed Wild Ennerdale. Now one of the UK's largest wildland partnerships, it is run by the Forestry Commission, the National Trust and United Utilities, with the

support of Natural England. These bodies work closely with the local people, who provide a large body of volunteers and have helped turn the valley into a living laboratory where there is no fixed goal, other than allowing natural processes to shape the landscape and ecology.

To achieve this, interventions are occasionally necessary to reverse the mistakes of the past. This includes the introduction of small numbers of Galloway cattle. These black, woolly creatures, known as 'Ennerdale bears', trample and disturb the ground, creating more diverse vegetation and blurring the old boundaries between forest and farmland.

The results have been spectacular, and in places where the cattle have been grazing for more than 10 years, a rich mosaic of habitats has been created, with trees such as birch, holly, larch and oak springing up alongside fruit-bearing trees and shrubs including juniper and bilberry. The number of birds in the valley has doubled, bolstered by a 65 per cent increase in the number of bird species. Together with its populations of otter, red squirrel, red and roe deer, and England's largest population of marsh fritillary butterflies, the River Liza hosts Britain's only migratory population of cold water Arctic char, an annual presence since the end of the last Ice Age around 12,000 years ago.

Mar Lodge Estate

The Rescue of a Wild Land

Wilderness, like beauty, lies in the eye of the beholder. Technically, it is defined as a landscape untouched by human hands. Appearances, however, can be deceptive. At first sight, the mountains, glens and heather-covered moorlands of the Scottish Highlands seem as near to a pristine wilderness as it is possible to get. In truth, their ancient woodlands have been deforested by man and over-browsed by red deer for many centuries.

This is why the recent history of the Mar Lodge Estate, located in the east of the Cairngorms National Park near Braemar in Aberdeenshire, is so compelling. In his book *Regeneration: The Rescue of a Wild Land* (2021), Andrew Painting, an ecologist at Mar Lodge, tells the story of how, since buying the estate in 1995, the National Trust for Scotland has regenerated the growth of Scots pine and brought the red deer population down to sustainable numbers.

Containing four of the five highest mountains in the UK, the estate is made up of over 1,100 sq. miles (almost 3,000 sq. km) of some of the most beautiful landscapes in Scotland, including moorland, Caledonian pine forest (the habitat of red squirrels and pine martens), 15 Munros (mountains over 3,000ft/914.4m) and the Quoich wetlands (home to wading birds and otters). More than 5,000 wildlife species live on the estate, including the golden eagle.

A more recent project has been to encourage the return of montane woodland, an ecologically important upland habitat that has been almost completely lost across Scotland due to fire and grazing. As a result, this is now steadily increasing across hundreds of acres of the estate and thousands more acres across the Cairngorms.

Mar Lodge has banned the practice of 'muirburn', in which huge areas of heather are burned to encourage the fresh shoots required to feed the quantity of young grouse needed for 'driven grouse shooting'. The latter involves the birds being flushed out of the undergrowth by 'beaters' for a large group of shooters. This has been replaced by 'walked-up shooting' where the grouse breed naturally and are shot in much smaller numbers by fewer shooters who flush out the birds themselves. This policy has already resulted in the return of the beautiful hen harrier to low-altitude moorland. Popularly known as the 'ghost of the moor' due to the male's predominantly pale grey plumage, hen harriers had previously suffered a massive decline in population due to their being shot by gamekeepers on the grouse moors to maintain grouse numbers.

Visitors to the Mar Lodge Estate can stay in the Victorian hunting lodge built by the first Duke of Fife and his wife, Princess Louise, Queen Victoria's granddaughter, both of whom are buried in the chapel adjoining the lodge. Queen Victoria herself laid the foundation stone to the lodge in 1895, while the Stag Ballroom, a listed building containing more than 2,430 stag heads dating from the 1800s to 1932, is a survivor from a long-lost era.

RSPB Minsmere Nature Reserve

Britain's Wildlife HQ

'There are certain places that seem to have been let off all the normal rules. Here the animals seem tamer, closer, more confiding; the rare ones seem to have become common, and human beings seem to have been granted a level of trust that they never have in the usual run of places.' So says the journalist and naturalist Simon Barnes of Minsmere, the RSPB's flagship nature reserve. And how could anyone disagree?

Minsmere, near Saxmundham on the coast of Suffolk, has been managed by the RSPB since 1947, soon after what had previously been agricultural land was flooded during the Second World War to deter a German invasion. Since then, it has become a byword for nature conservation, and

home to many of the rarer species of birds and mammals profiled in this book. These include ospreys, nightingales, bitterns, otters, water voles and natterjack toads.

Most significant among them in the history of Minsmere, however, is the avocet, a wader famous for its black and white plumage and distinctive upturned beak, which bred here for the first time shortly after the war following an interval of more than a century. This accelerated the RSPB's decision to lease, and later buy, the land, with the avocet subsequently being chosen to be the emblem of the RSPB.

The architect of Minsmere's international reputation today was its first full-time warden, the legendary Bert Axell. Axell was essentially a visionary 'rewilder' – decades before the term was invented – who understood the importance of helping to create habitats that would support rare species before letting nature do the rest.

To this end, he designed Minsmere's famous Scrape, creating an area of shallow ponds studded with islands while carefully controlling water levels and salinity to mimic a natural saline lagoon. While still needing careful management, his vision has resulted in a bonanza of nesting waders, terns and gulls.

A key part of Minsmere's appeal lies in the mosaic of wildlife habitats that make up its 2,470 acres (1,000ha). Its mix of woodlands and wetlands, reedbeds, lowland heath, marshland, coastal scrub and shingle beach have helped it become a biodiversity hotspot, with more than 5,800 species recorded. It also proved to be a highly popular and productive base for the BBC's *Springwatch* team for three years, from 2014 to 2016.

Minsmere has also established a well-deserved reputation as one of the most welcoming wildlife sites to visit, whatever your level of knowledge. It has an excellent visitor centre and eight hides complemented by a team of knowledgeable guides and volunteers to help with identification and general information. Its walking trails follow routes through all its many different habitats, and there is also a Discovery Centre, Wild Zone and Wild Wood Adventure area, where the young and young-at-heart can build a den.

Addresses

Alladale Wilderness Reserve
Ardgay, Sutherland, IV24 3BS
(see pp.180–3)

Arlington Court (National Trust)
Arlington, near Barnstaple, Devon,
EX31 4LP
(see p.33)

Blakeney National Nature Reserve
(National Trust)
Morston Quay, Quay Road, Morston,
Norfolk, NR25 7BH
(see pp.12, 166–9)

Blickling Estate
(National Trust)
Blickling Estate, Aylsham, Norfolk,
NR11 6NF
(see p.107)

Brownsea Island
(National Trust)
Poole Harbour, Poole, Dorset, BH13 7EE
(see pp.19, 145, 162–5)

Clattinger Farm (Wiltshire Wildlife Trust)
Lower Moor, Oaksey, Near Cricklade,
Wiltshire, SN16 9TW
(see pp.114–5)

Crom (National Trust)
Upper Lough Erne, Newtownbutler, County
Fermanagh, BT92 8AJ
(see pp.19, 37)

Dinefwr (National Trust)
Dinefwr Park, Newton House, Llandeilo,
Carmarthenshire, SA19 6RT
(see p.33)

Donna Nook National Nature Reserve
(Lincolnshire Wildlife Trust)
Marsh Lane, Donna Nook, Louth, LN11 7PD
(see p.13)

Egleton Nature Reserve
Egleton, Oakham, Rutland, LE15 8BT
(see p.173)

Emmetts Garden (National Trust)
Ide Hill, Sevenoaks, Kent, TN14 6BA
(see p.107)

Gigrin Farm – Red Kite Feeding and
Rehabilitation Centre
South Street, Rhayader, Powys, LD6 5BL
(see pp.61)

Gilfach Nature Reserve (Radnorshire
Wildlife Trust)
St. Harmon, Rhayader, Powys, LD6 5LF
(see p.149)

Glenfeshie Estate
Kincraig, Cairngorms National Park,
PH21 1NX
(see pp.188–91)

Glenloy Wildlife
Glenloy Lodge, Banavie, Fort William,
PH33 7PD
(see p.37)

Ham Wall Nature Reserve (RSPB)
Meare, Ashcott, Glastonbury, BA6 9SX
(see pp.45, 65)

Holkham National Nature Reserve
Holkham Hall, Wells-next-the-Sea, Norfolk,
NR23 1AB
(see p.101)

Holme Dunes National Nature Reserve
(Norfolk Wildlife Trust)
Broadwater Road, Hunstanton, PE36 6LQ
(see p.139)

Insh Marshes Nature Reserve (RSPB)
Kingussie, PH21 1NT
(see pp.174–7)

Knepp Estate
Knepp Castle, West Grinstead, West Sussex,
RH13 8LJ
(see pp.21, 31, 184–7)

Lakenheath Fen Nature Reserve (RSPB)
Station Rd, Lakenheath, Brandon, Thetford,
Suffolk, IP27 9AD
(see p.65)

Lackford Lakes Nature Reserve (Suffolk
Wildlife Trust)
Lackford Lakes, Bury St Edmunds, Suffolk,
IP28 6HX
(see p.75)

Leighton Moss Nature Reserve (RSPB)
Myers Farm, Storrs Lane, Silverdale,
Carnforth, LA5 0SW
(see pp.25, 45, 89, 99)

Loch Garten Nature Reserve (RSPB)
Abernethy National Nature Reserve, Forest
Lodge, Nethy Bridge, PH25 3EF
(see p.56)

London Wetland Centre (WWT)
Queen Elizabeth Walk, Barnes, London,
SW13 9WT
(see pp.75, 99)

Lyme (National Trust)
Disley, Stockport, Cheshire, SK12 2NR
(see pp.27, 33)

Lyndon Nature Reserve (Leicestershire
and Rutland Wildlife Trust)
Lyndon Road, Manton, Rutland, LE15 8RN
(see p.173)

Malham Tarn (National Trust)
Waterhouses, Settle, North Yorkshire,
BD24 9PT
(see pp.146–7)

Mar Lodge Estate (National Trust for
Scotland)
Braemar, Ballater, AB35 5YJ
(see pp.196–7)

Minsmere Nature Reserve (RSPB)
Sheepwash Lane, Saxmundham, IP17 3BY
(see pp.25, 27, 88, 99, 198–201)

Mount Stewart (National Trust)
Portaferry Road, Newtownards, County
Down, BT22 2AD
(see pp.19, 115)

North Harris Eagle Observatory
Glen, Meavaig, Isle of Harris, HS3 3AW
(see p.55)

Plas yn Rhiw (National Trust)
Rhiw, Pwllheli, Gwynedd, LL53 8AB
(see p.107)

Rainham Marshes Nature Reserve (RSPB)
New Tank Hill Rd, Purfleet, Essex,
RM19 1SZ
(see p.147)

Runnymede and Ankerwycke (National
Trust)
Windsor Road, near Old Windsor, Surrey,
SL4 2JL
(see p.111)

Rutland Water Nature Reserve
(Leicestershire and Rutland Wildlife Trust)
Oakham, LE15 8BT
(see pp.56, 57, 170–3)

Rydal Mount
Ambleside, Lake District, LA22 9LU
(see p.133)

Rye Meads Nature Reserve (RSPB)
Rye Road, Hoddesdon, Hertfordshire,
SG12 8JS
(see p.75)

**Sandscale Haws National
Nature Reserve**
Roanhead, Hawthwaite Lane, near Barrow-
in-Furness, Cumbria, LA14 4QJ
(see pp.138–9)

Scottish Dolphin Centre (WDC)
Spey Bay, Moray, IV32 7PJ
(see p.153)

Scottish Seabird Centre
North Berwick, EH39 4SS
(see p.76)

Sheffield Park and Garden (National Trust)
Sheffield Park, Uckfield, East Sussex,
TN22 3QX
(see p.107)

Sheringham Park (National Trust)
Upper Sheringham, Norfolk, NR26 8TL
(see p.125)

Slimbridge Wetland Centre (WWT)
Bowditch, Slimbridge, Gloucestershire,
GL2 7BT
(see p.45)

Snettisham Nature Reserve (RSPB)
Beach Road, Snettisham, King's Lynn,
PE31 7RA
(see pp.85, 89 and 101)

Spurn Bird Observatory
Easington Road, Kilnsea, Hull, HU12 0UB
(see p.85)

**Staveley Nature Reserve (Yorkshire
Wildlife Trust)**
Minskip Road, Boroughbridge, HG5 9LQ
(see p.75)

Stourhead (National Trust)
Near Mere, Wiltshire, BA12 6QD
(see p.121)

**Threave Garden & Estate (National Trust
for Scotland)**
Castle Douglas, DG7 1RX
(see p.151)

Tyntesfield (National Trust)
Wraxall, Bristol, North Somerset, BS48 1NX
(see p.125)

**Westonbirt, The National Arboretum
(Forestry England)**
Tetbury, GL8 8QS
(see p.121)

**Wicken Fen Nature Reserve
(National Trust)**
Lode Lane, Wicken, Ely, Cambridgeshire,
CB7 5XP
(see pp.45, 160–1)

**Wild Ennerdale (National Trust/Forestry
England/Natural England/United Utilities)**
Peil Wyke, Bassenthwaite Lake, CA13 9YG
(see pp.192–5)

Wild Ken Hill
Heacham Bottom Farm, Lynn Road,
Snettisham, PE31 7PQ
(see pp.96–97)

Wimpole Estate (National Trust)
Arrington, Royston, Cambridgeshire,
SG8 0BW
(see p.27)

Winkworth Arboretum (National Trust)
Hascombe Road, Godalming, Surrey,
GU8 4AD
(see p.121)

Woolsthorpe Manor (National Trust)
Water Lane, Woolsthorpe by Colsterworth,
Grantham, Lincolnshire, NG33 5PD
(see p.111)

Picture Credits

Index